ATHENS AND ATTICA

PRODUCTION COORDINATOR: Athina Ragia

ENGLISH TRANSLATION: Alexandra Doumas

PROOF READING: Ifigeneia Stefanou

EDITOR OF GREEK TEXTS: Kiki Birtacha

CARTOGRAPHY: Kelly Kalogirou

REPRODUCTION OF ILLUSTRATIONS: Nikos Alexiades

ISBN 978 960 204 337 0

58 Skoufa Street, 10680 Athens, Greece
Tel. +30 210 3611692, Fax +30 210 3600865
www.melissabooks.com

Printed and bound in Greece

Athens and Attica

HISTORY AND ARCHAEOLOGY

EDITOR
Andreas G. Vlachopoulos

MELISSA PUBLISHING HOUSE

Contents

Prehistoric Times

OLGA KAKAVOGIANNI

THE STONE AGE (40,000–3000 BC) | At least 40,000 years ago, during the final period of the Palaeolithic Age, man was present in Attica, in the mountains and the small plains, the forests and the vales, where there was a plenteous food supply and there were many caves for refuge. At the southern end of the region, in the Kitsos cave overlooking Lavrion (anc. Laurion), a few stone tools and traces of a makeshift dwelling, as well as a weapon tip from the Vravona cave and a chopping tool from Pyrinna, Spata, attest his activity. Future research will reveal his traces at other sites that the archaeologist's pick will bring to light.

By the Early Neolithic period (7th/6th millennium BC), 34,000 years later, the nomadic hunters and gatherers of the caves have already become tillers of the soil, capable "architects" and builders, who wisely choose their place of settlement near the coast or streams, organize the space of their settlements and construct their small houses intended for one family, not only with wattle and daub [fig. 3], but also with excellent stone masonry, as ascertained in the settlement southwest of Pallini, beside the Attica Highway (*Attiki Odos*) [fig. 4], and at Yalou, Spata, byside the small habitations at Merenda, Kalyvia, Kifissia. They know too how to find water by sinking deep wells, how to cultivate and to produce their dietary staples (wheat, legumes, dairy produce and meat from domesticated sheep and goats), and how to keep them in small well-built storerooms. They have become skilled potters, making vases for everyday needs, and modellers of anthropomorphic figurines [fig. 1], cult symbols or simple toys, as well as knappers who supplied the community with tools of hard stones, flint, or obsidian brought from the distant island of Melos, which they reached in small sea craft already from the ninth millennium BC.

Social and cultural developments during the fifth millennium BC (Late Neolithic period) were rapid. By now, Attica was inhabited systematically, in installations in caves or in the countryside, as is deduced from the remains identified at many sites in eastern Attica, the Attica basin and the plain of Elefsina (anc. Eleusis). Building remains from this period are scant. On the contrary, in the caves which offered safe and pleasant living conditions, due

1

1 Pallini. Clay male figurine of the Early Neolithic period (early 6th millennium BC). Brauron Archaeological Museum.

to the stable temperature of their interior, the remnants of human life have been preserved undisturbed. These bear witness to remarkable skills in making vases, plain and burnished or decorated, tools, anthropomorphic and zoomorphic figurines and symbols, as well as in weaving and sewing. At Pousi Kalogeri, in the area of Vravrona (anc. Brauron) and at Merenda, in the caves of Pan at Marathon, Leontari on Hymettos, Kitsos at Lavrion [fig. 2], Keratea, as well as Rizoupoli in the Athens basin, the finds are abundant.

Towards the end of the Neolithic Age, in the fourth millennium BC, the inhabitants of Attic started to utilize a new material, which they found initially in its natural state, native copper. Subsequently, they learnt how to extract the metal from cupiferous ores, just as they possibly obtained silver from argentiferous lead, which was extracted from plumbiferous ores. By the end of this phase, at least, it is certain that they began to exploit the metalliferous lodes of the Laureotike. The hilltops where these levels were accessible were filled with small settlements, such as at Thorikos, obviously of miners who opened small mining galleries, which were later widened, as is the case with gallery 3 at Thorikos.

In the closing centuries of the Neolithic Age (late 4th millennium BC) a new type of dwelling appeared at Merenda, consisting of clusters of underground chambers cut in the soft bedrock [fig. 5].

Man's beliefs about death can be discerned vaguely in the Neolithic Age. It is strange that even in areas where extensive and complete research has been conducted, in the form of field surveys and excavations (Early Neolithic settlements at Nea Makri, Pallini and Merenda, as well as other settlements of the Final Neolithic period, also at Merenda), no cemeteries have been found. However, a few isolated graves have come to light: one grave of the sixth millennium BC in the Pallini plain and two graves of the fourth millennium BC, one in the ancient Agora of Athens, in an underground chamber, and the other in the cave of Pan.

Maritime communications seem to have been well developed, mainly with the Cyclades. Obsidian was brought from Melos in sea craft that voyaged from island to island, which at that time were closer to one another, because sea level was some four to five metres lower than it is today.

2

2 Lavrion, Kitsos cave. Vase with painted geometric motifs. Late Neolithic period (5th millennium BC). Lavrion Archaeological Museum.

THE BRONZE AGE (3000–1000 BC) | The era after the mid-fourth millennium BC and spanning the third and second millennia BC is characterized by the use of metals and mainly bronze, after which it was named. The use of bronze to make durable tools and weapons gave great momentum to the development of society and culture. Metallurgy, which, as the metallurgical workshop for cupellation of argentiferous lead at Lambrika near Koropi and

3 Restoration drawing of a hut of the Early Neolithic period (7th/6th millennium BC), from the settlement excavated at Nea Makri.

4 Pallini. Remains of three Neolithic houses in the settlement at Pallini, which is dated to the Early Neolithic period.

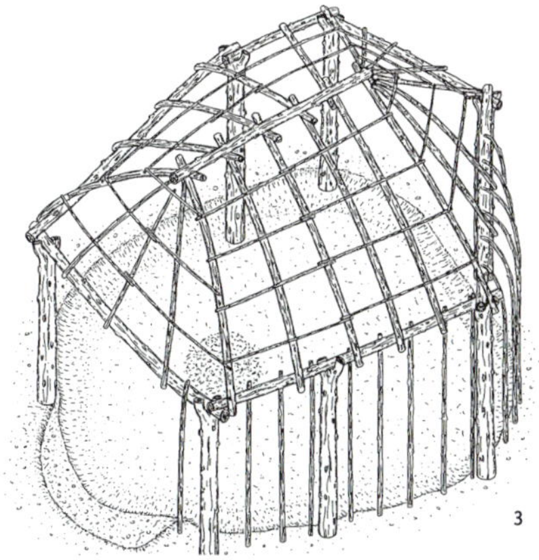

3

4

5

5 Merenda. Underground rock-cut chambers. Visible are the entrance and two main rooms of these peculiar dwellings of the Final Neolithic period (late 4th millennium BC).

6

6 Koropi. Vase with undulating rim and dense linear decoration in successive zones, from the settlement excavated at Koropi. After mid-3rd millennium BC. Brauron Archaeological Museum.

the pit with scoriae at Rafina have revealed, was practised systematically, presupposes specialization of labour, promotes trade and contributes to the accumulation of wealth and possibly to the incipient formation of economic-social classes, as well as to the establishment of strong central authority.

Already from the early third millennium BC (Early Helladic period) these phenomena can be detected in the population increase, which is attested by the incremental rise in the number of sites with settlement remains, from Oropos to as far as the Elefsina plain and Sounion. The large settlements at Rafina and nearby Askitario, at Magoula of Spata, Koropi [fig. 6] and Agios Kosmas, have sophisticated organization and architecture, with high density of building, streets and squares, and in some cases separate "neighbourhoods", while the buildings were roofed with clay tiles. Some settlements were protected by an enclosure or enceinte (Agreliki of Marathon, Rafina, Askitario [figs 10, 11], Agios Kosmas, Koropi), but only the settlement on Zagani hill at Spata is surrounded by a strong wall, making it a small but true citadel [fig. 7]. Large underground rock-cut chambers continued to be created too, as at Koropi, which were used possibly only as storerooms and not as dwellings, as in earlier times at Merenda.

The numerous moveable finds bear witness to a population with refined aesthetic taste. The household equipment consists of large clay hearths, many four-legged vessels, copious vases of diverse new shapes and decoration, made for consuming olive oil and wine. These were produced in large quantities, testifying on the one hand to a society with a comfortable life style and on the other to the ability and creativity of its craftsmen [figs 5, 8, 10, 11].

Progress in man's existence is also reflected in aspects of his spiritual life. Great care is lavished on the dead, as is ascertained from the large cemeteries, such as the extensive and strictly organized burial ground at Tsepi of Marathon, where there are small, built family graves with conventional *dromos* and doorway [fig. 9], on the coast of Glyfada, at Agios Kosmas, at Markopoulo, as well as in the tombs of a type that appears for the first time, with an underground rock-cut chamber, which have been found in Athens (Olympieion) and Nea Makri. The graves are the new home of the dead, in which they are accompanied by many objects used in their daily life (vases, jewellery and figurines) and receive ritual offerings, perhaps also of food.

Furthermore, the discovery of sites with offerings on the summits of mountains, such as Hymettos, must be associated with faith in supreme natural powers, as is the case in the contemporary peak sanctuaries of Crete. Such sites have been found on Mount Hymettos, as well as possibly on the Acropolis, where a level of Early Helladic objects was found under the sanctuary of Pandrosos. The relatively abundant clay figurines of bovines and the marble female figurines of Cycladic type, which are found in graves as well as in settlements, may be linked with the expression of religious beliefs. The marble figurines, together with several other items of Cycladic material culture, such as "frying-pan" vessels [fig. 8], indicate the close relations between Attica and the Cyclades. Last, it is noteworthy that for some peculiar buildings of the Early Helladic period, the apsidal buildings at Akadimia Platonos (Plato's Academy) in Athens and the area of the large ancient temple at Merenda, or their locus, particular care and respect was shown in historical times, a fact that could perhaps be interpreted as honouring illustrious ancestors.

After a flourishing lasting almost eight hundred years, a decline commenced in Attica, evidenced by differences in the picture of habitation and in elements of everyday life. These changes were intensified at the dawn of the second millennium BC. The period known as Middle Helladic had perhaps begun before 2000 BC and presents marked differentiation in the settlement pattern of the region, since there is a drastic reduction in the number of settlements and a degeneration of the material culture, in relation to the pre-

7 Spata, Zagani. General view of the fortified settlement of the early 3rd millennium BC. The settlement was excavated in the course of works on the new Athens airport at Spata. The building remains were dismantled and the hill was razed, since it was decided that it impeded the safe flight of aircraft. A relief model of the settlement and finds from it are exhibited in the Museum of the Eleftherios Venizelos International Airport.

7

8

8 Tsepi, Marathon. Clay "frying-pan" vessels with impressed decoration of spirals and conventional representation of the solar disc at the centre. First half of the 3rd millennium BC. Marathon Archaeological Museum.

9 At Tsepi, Marathon an extensive cemetery of the end of the 4th millennium BC and the begining of the 3rd millennium BC (Early Bronze Age) has been excavated, yielding assorted types of family graves and grave goods, many of which reveal strong influences from the contemporary Cycladic Culture. The archaeological site is preserved under a modern shelter and is open to the public.

9

10, 11 Rafina. Sauce-boat (left) and jug (right) from the Early Helladic settlement at Askitario, Rafina. Mid-3rd millennium BC. Athens, National Archaeological Museum.

12 Aphidnai. Triple vase, a characteristic example of grey "Minyan" ware of the Middle Helladic period (2000–1600 BC), from the Aphidnai tumulus. Athens, National Archaeological Museum.

13 Plasi, Marathon. Jug of the late Middle Helladic period (1700–1600 BC), with bichrome representation of a bird with outspread wings and turning its head backwards. Marathon Archaeological Museum.

10

11

vious splendid period. Nevertheless, alongside the decrease in the number of settlements, some settlements expanded in size: Thorikos, Agios Nikolaos in Anavyssos, Kephale (pres. Keratea), Lamptrai, Sphettos (pres. Koropi), Brauron (pres. Vravrona), Marathon (pres. Plasi [fig. 13] and Agreliki), Athens, Eleusis (pres. Elefsina), while during the same period others were created, such as the fortified citadel at Aphidnai. This concentration of population perhaps confirms in reality the first synoecism of Attica, which is attributed to its mythical "first king", Kekrops the Diphyes or dual-natured (Strabo, *Geography* 9.1.20). These small towns (*komai*) will have been the seats of local rulers, perhaps the first "kings", linked in tradition with specific names.

No settlements of this period have been excavated, just a few small houses at Brauron, Thorikos and on the south slope of the Acropolis, and knowledge of the architecture is therefore limited. Despite the paucity of evidence, it can be argued that several Middle Helladic sites, apart from the peak sanctuary on Hymettos, developed into large or smaller shrines in Mycenaean times or later in historical times: the Erechtheion [fig. 69], the temple of Artemis Tauropolos at Loutsa, the temenos at Merenda, the "heroon of Kranaos" at Lamptrai, the temple of Artemis Mounichia in the Piraeus, at Rafina. These sites are frequently associated in later times with a local deity or with the eponymous hero of the area and are a clear indication that ancestor cult was practised towards the end of the prehistoric era and at the beginning of historical times.

Furthermore, the creation of family funerary tumuli (three at Vranas of Marathon, a rectangular one on the south slope of the Acropolis and a large one at Aphidnai [fig. 12]), where other graves developed around a central burial, suggests that the great clans of Attica were already being formed.

12

13

14 Thorikos. Mycenaean tholos tomb (13th c. BC) on the citadel of Thorikos. These monumental constructions comprise a circular chamber and a long dromos, and are associated with rulers or powerful local lords. Similar tombs in Attica have been found at Acharnai (Menidi) and Marathon.

15 Glyka Nera. Mycenaean figurine of three figures, from Fouresi (14th c. BC). Represented are two females (*kourotrophoi*) holding a child on their shoulders. Brauron Archaeological Museum.

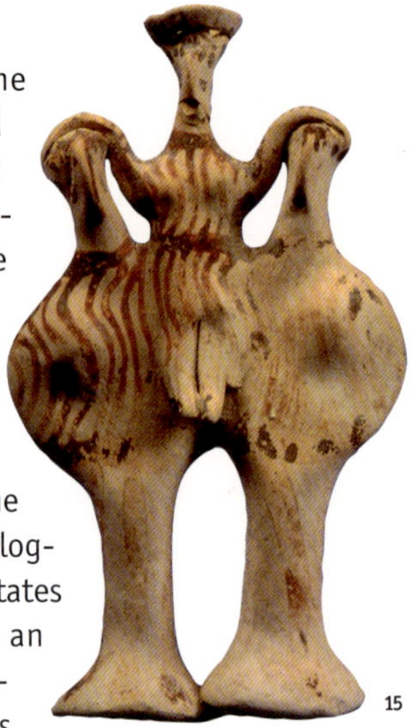

15

Many technological achievements, such as the wide use of the potter's wheel, which contributed to the progress in vase-making [figs 12, 13], and the now advanced metallurgy, with the production of alloys, spread rapidly and prepared the way for the major cultural floruit of the succeeding centuries, which is associated with the Mycenaean Civilization (1600–1100 BC).

The epic tradition passed down into historical times, the first texts, written on clay tablets in the archives of the Mycenaean palaces, and archaeological finds, inform us of the existence of small states with a well-structured administration and an organized army and navy. As a result of specialized fabrication of goods, extensive overseas trade and the founding of stations for mercantile transactions (*emporia*), which reached to the ends of the Mediterranean and perhaps to the Euxine Pontus, these states accumulated wealth and acquired political power, which is manifested either in the expansion of their sovereignty to neighbouring ones, or in the undertaking of overseas ventures and campaigns, such as the Voyage of the Argonauts and the Trojan War.

The pronounced mobility and the contacts with neighbouring populations or with the goods and the ideas of far-off peoples provided opportunities for exchanging technological know-how and artistic conventions, as the rich finds attest. After an interim phase during which the old (Middle Helladic) cultural elements continued in existence while the new ones were infiltrating, Attica was included fully in the sphere of influence of the Mycenaean world (Late Helladic period).

14

First Thorikos, where there is unbroken habitation from the Final Neolithic period, presents clear indications of power and wealth, which were due to the exploitation of the mines in the Laureotike. Here, already in the early phase of the Mycenaean period (1600–1400 BC), the first big tholos tombs [fig. 14] in Attica were founded for the local lords, while built cist graves with entrance, covered by a tumulus, were also in use. The dead were accompanied by fine vases, precious jewellery and even decorated lead balance weights.

However, this wealth seems to have provoked the envy and the intervention of the Minoans, masters of the seas, and perhaps the tribute that the Athenians sent to Minos, and from which obligation Theseus liberated them, was associated with the Laurion mines. With the uniting of the various small villages under a single administration, the "synoecism", the hero became founder of the Athenian State. This appears as a single state in the Homeric

16

16 Spata. Ivory comb with intricate decoration of sphinxes, from the chamber tomb at Spata, in which rulers were most probably buried (14th c. BC). Athens, National Archaeological Museum.

17 Shoe-shaped ritual vases (rhyta) from chamber tombs at Alyki, Voula [fig. 17b] and Pikermi [fig. 17a] dated to the 14th c. BC. The painted wings on the side of the model from Alyki are most probably associated with the journey of the deceased to the Netherworld. Athens, National Archaeological Museum.

"List of Ships" that took part in the Trojan Campaign (*Iliad* II 546–556), in which Athens participated with 50 vessels, under the command of Theseus's successor, Menestheus.

In this period Athens, the "well-built citadel" the "ἐϋκτίμενον πτολίεθρον" of Homer, acquired particular importance. A large building, the "palace", seems to have been founded upon the Acropolis, while shortly before 1200 BC this was fortified with a mighty wall, parts of which survive to the south of the Propylaia and under the tower of the temple of Athena Nike [fig. 88]. It was then that the descent to the north fountain was constructed, at a great depth in a fissure in the rock, and was included *intra muros*. Perhaps the palace was also locus of worship of Athena, while a small building of this period, to the north of the Erechtheion, is linked with the worship of Erechtheus. Scant remnants of habitation have survived from the Mycenaean period, mainly on the south slope of the Acropolis and in the wider area of the Agora. By contrast, many underground, rock-cut chamber tombs and simpler graves have come to light, the dead in which were accompanied by rich grave goods: painted vases, jewellery, ivories. One such tomb was excavated on the north side of the Areios Pagos (Areopagus) hill.

In rural Attica, in addition to Thorikos other large centres emerged, such as Pallini (anc. Pallene), seat of the mythical Pallas, brother and rival of Aegeus, Marathon and Eleusis, while many smaller ones were established in the Mesogeia and the Athens basin. The settlements continued to grow at the sites of Middle Helladic villages, and indeed some of them (Aphidnai, Eleusis, Lamptrai) were surrounded by a wall. No systematic excavations of Mycenaean settlements have been conducted, which is why little is known about their urban plan and organization.

17 a

17 b

18

18, 19 Marathon. Shallow cup (phiale) of beaten gold sheet (Athens, National Archaeological Museum), from the tholos tomb at Marathon [fig. 19], in the dromos of which preceded a ceremonial burial of the two horses that had drawn the chariot with the body of the deceased.

20, 21 Perati (Porto Rafti). Vases from the Mycenaean cemetery at Perati. On the rim of the lekanis or kalathos [fig. 20] are clay figurines of lamenting females, precursory types of corresponding figurines of the Geometric period. The stirrup jar [fig. 21] is painted with close decoration of octopus, fish and birds, and is a characteristic vase of the 12th century BC. Athens, National Archaeological Museum.

19

Around the settlements, large community cemeteries have been found, usually of chamber tombs, at Chamolia-Lapoutsi near Vravrona, at Vourvatsi (anc. Lamptrai), at Magoula of Spata, Fouresi of Glyka Nera [fig. 15], in the environs of ancient Pallene, at Glyfada, Varkiza, Voula and Elefsina (anc. Eleusis). Smaller cemeteries dispersed in the countryside, at sites where no settlements have been identified, are perhaps family burial grounds close to patrimonial landholdings. Usually the dead are accompanied by many grave goods, mainly vases, jewellery weapons and figurines.

Special mention should be made of the continuous use of the tumuli at Marathon, as well as the creation of new ones. At a short distance from these, a large tholos tomb was constructed, the grave goods recovered from which include a gold cup [fig. 18], while the horses of the funerary chariot had been interred in the *dromos* [fig. 19]. Two rich chamber tombs at Spata, although looted, yielded hundreds of pieces of jewellery and other objects of gold and ivory [fig. 16], such as a lyre with relief decoration, and a boar's-tusk helmet. At Fouresi of Glyka Nera, Minoan artefacts were found in a large chamber tomb with long *dromos*. The big tholos tomb south of Menidi contained many precious grave goods and one Canaanite amphora from Palestine. In the West Cemetery at Eleusis, large built cist graves with entrance were excavated. One part of the cemetery had been delimited by an enclosure in Antiquity and was never used again, perhaps constituting the cemetery in which the ancient Eleusinians pointed out the tombs of the "Seven against Thebes", that is of the seven Argeian generals who, under the leadership of Polyneikes, exiled son of Oedipus, and of Adrastos, king of Argos, campaigned against Thebes (which was ruled by Oedipus' other son, Eteokles), where they were slain.

Evidence that can be related to religious beliefs is rare. Nonetheless, several sites at which acts of worship took place have been identified on the basis of the presence of vases for libations, models of footwear [fig. 17a–b] and zoomorphic and schematic anthropomorphic figurines. Some sites are the same as those used for worship in the Middle Helladic period, and at most of them worship continued into historical times. So, with the exception of the sanctuary on the summit of Hymettos, a Mycenaean megaron perhaps used for cult has been found beneath the sacred Telesterion of Eleusis [fig. 127], Mycenaean pottery was recovered from under the temple of Artemis Mounichia and of Artemis Tauropolos, and the temple of Apollo Delios at Prasiai. An open-air sanctuary has been identified on the east slope of the acropolis of Lamptrai.

20

Civilization flourished during Mycenaean times, the output of the pottery workshops burgeoned and the mercantile ships voyaged to the Syro-Palestinian shores. The Laurion mines were fully operational, supplying southern Greece and the Aegean with silver (*so-Fe-no* = *sounos* of the Mycenaean tablets in Linear B script) and lead, and perhaps an attempt was made to open other mines on Hymettos, in the vicinity of Sphettos.

In the early twelfth century BC, the period following the collapse of the Mycenaean palatial system, a gradual decline is observed, without any sign of violent or martial episodes. This fact reinforces the tradition that the Athenians repulsed the advance of the so-called Dorian tribes. And whereas all the settlements started to shrink and habitation continued only around the Acropolis, as indicated by the large cemetery of 100 graves in the Kerameikos [fig. 58], one large and important centre appeared at the harbour of Prasiai on the east coast of Attica.

At the site of Perati, opposite the islet of Raftis, an extensive cemetery of 220 tombs, most of them family chamber tombs, has been excavated, while recently a second cemetery has been found a short way to the west, in the environs of ancient Steiria. The settlement that the two cemeteries served has not been located, but from the rich and varied grave goods it is clear that they belonged to a flourishing community of seafarers and merchants, which obtained precious and exotic objects from distant land samulets, scarabs and cartouches with the name of the Pharaoh Ramses II from Egypt, and cylinder seals from Syria. Of the more than 1,300 vases recovered, characteristic are those decorated with standardized representations of octopuses [fig. 21], as well as a few on which the rendering is freer, which are products of local workshops [fig. 20].

After Mycenaean times (that is, after 1100 BC), life in Attica seems to have dwindled and only a few finds bear witness to its continuation. These are mainly a few vases of the Protogeometric period (10th century BC), found in cemeteries primarily of the Geometric period (Athens [fig. 57], Nea Ionia, Acharnai, Eleusis, Koropi, Rafina, Thorikos) or singly. Obviously the splendid and glorious Mycenaean world of heroes and palaces, sung of by Homer, existed no more and another world, conservative but dynamic, was rising, the world of tilling the soil, hymned by Hesiod in his *Works and Days* in the seventh century BC.

21

Historical Times:

from the Geometric period (10th century BC) to Late Antiquity (6th century AD)

ANGELOS P. MATTHAIOU

The mountains Aigaleo, Parnes, Pentele and Hymettos rim the Athens basin, leaving free its exit to the sea, while cutting it off from the rest of Attica, mainly the regions west of Aigaleo and east of Hymettos, save for a few passes towards these [fig. 25]. The geomorphology of Attica distinguished it into three large entities, the city (*asty*), the coast (*paralia*) and the interior (*mesogaia*), and made a decisive contribution to the creation of small towns which were independent and administratively autonomous, the *tetrakomiai*, e.g. of Marathon, or that around the "*tetrakomon Herakleion*" in the Piraeus. This reality is reflected in an ancient testimony, recorded by Strabo (*Geography* 9.1.20), that Kekrops, the mythical king of Athens, was responsible for the first synoecism of the s mall towns of Athens into twelve cities. In the long history of the city-state of Athens, Attica was its rural territory (*chora*) and consequently the history of Attica is articulated absolutely with that of Athens.

The Athenians believed that the political synoecism of all the towns (*komai*) dispersed throughout Attica was due to Theseus [fig. 22]. This common conviction is expressed by Thucydides (2.15.1–3), who writes: "... For in the time of Cecrops and the earliest kings down to Theseus, Attica had been divided into separate towns, each with its own town hall and magistrates, and so long as they had nothing to fear they did not come together to consult with the king, but separately administered their own affairs and took counsel for themselves. Sometimes they even made war upon the king, as, for example, the Eleusinians under Eumolpus did against Erechtheus of Athens. But when Theseus became king and proved himself a powerful as well as a prudent ruler, he not only reorganized the country in other respects, but abolished the councils and magistracies of the minor towns and brought all their inhabitants into union with what is now the city, establishing a single council and town hall, and compelled them, while continuing to occupy each his own lands as before, to use Athens as the sole

22

22 Attic red-figure kylix, attributed to the Elpinikos Painter. Depicted in the tondo is the Labour of Theseus against Sines the Pityokamptes. *Ca* 490 BC. Munich, Staatliche Antikensammlungen.

capital. This became a great city, since all were now paying their taxes to it, and was such when Theseus handed it down to his successors. And from his time even to this day the Athenians have celebrated at the public expense a festival called the Synoecia, in honour of the goddess" [Transl. C.F. Smith, Loeb Classical Library]. Theseus was in fact considered the founder-hero (*oikistes*) of the city, which is why when Kimon brought the hero's remains from Skyros, in 476/5 BC, they were buried with great honours in the Agora "in the middle of the city", as Plutarch writes (*Theseus* 36.4), as other cities did for their *oikistai*.

However, in view of modern historical research the attributing of the synoecism of Athens to Theseus is an anachronism. The archaeological evidence shows that it is highly unlikely that the synoecism took place at the end of the Bronze Age (14th–12th centuries BC), to which the reign of Theseus is dated. If it had occurred so early, it is almost impossible that it would have survived in the years following the end of the Mycenaean world, when, as the excavation data show, many settlements shrank or were abandoned and a large part of the Attic countryside was deserted. On the basis of the archaeological evidence, the synoecism is dated after the tenth century BC, during the so-called Dark Age.

The prevailing of Athens made the city's king sole sovereign, who for at least two hundred years ruled it together with a council of nobles. However, it seems that royal power had been curbed already by the second half of the eighth century BC. By the end of the sixth century BC the king lost almost all his competences, except in the domain of cult, and his authority became annual but was never abolished. Nonetheless, the Athenians considered that their last king, who held the old form of the office, was Kodros [fig. 24], whose reign is dated to the eleventh century BC. Legend has it that when the Dorians invaded Attica, Kodros, knowing the Delphic oracle they had received, according to which they would succeed if they did not kill the Athenian king, decided to sacrifice himself in order to save his homeland.

The curbing of royal power was a consequence of the increasing might of the nobles, the *aristoi*, who came from the great clans or lineages which owned most of the land. The government of the city was based on descent and land ownership. The three principal archons the eponymous, the *polemarchos* and the *basileus*, and the *boule* of the *Areios Pagos* (Areopagus), the ruling magistrates, came from the ranks of the *aristoi*. Alongside the great clans lived the mass of the population, ordinary farmers and artisans, most of them working on the big estates and frequently deep in debt, who were excluded from the administration of the city. Continuous borrowing on swingeing terms ended in the debtors passing into slavery, since credit with the person as collateral was allowed. The abject situation of *hoi polloi* possibly led to rebellion and perhaps a consequence of this was the attempt by

23

23 Red-figure oinochoe, *ca* 400 BC. Depicted is the statue group of the tyrannicides, Harmodios and Aristogeiton. Boston, Museum of Fine Arts.

24 Athens. In the place where the Peloponnesians assassinated Kodros, close to the Panathenaic Stadium (Pausanias, *Attica* 19.5), the Athenians had set up a funerary monument, at some time unknown. Found not far from there, near the monument of Lysikrates, in the 19th century, was a partially preserved commemorative epigram of the late 1st century BC, which had been erected on Kodros' tomb at that time. Athens, Epigraphical Museum.

25 Aerial view of the Athens basin. In the background the mountains Hymettos, Pentele, Parnes and Aigaleo, and in the foreground the shoreline of Piraeus.

24

25

26

27

26, 27 Athens. The inscribed crowning of an altar **[fig. 26]** was found in 1877 to the southwest of the sanctuary of Zeus Olympios, between it and the right bank of the River Ilissos. The altar (**fig. 27**, restored) was dedicated in the sanctuary of Apollo Pythios, beside the Olympieion, by Peisistratos son of Hippias, grandson and namesake of the tyrant, who served as eponymous archon of Athens (possibly in 522/1 BC). The monument existed in the time of Thucydides (6.54.6-7), who records the full text of the inscription. Athens, Epigraphical Museum.

the Athenian nobleman and Olympic victor Kylon (632 BC?) to seize power and become tyrant. With the help of the Megarians he captured the Acropolis, but the Athenians reacted and the attempted coup failed. Kylon escaped but the other conspirators were put to the sword, despite assurances to the contrary. The Alkmeonides, a renowned clan of Athens, were considered responsible and were banished. Not long after (*ca* 621 BC), Drakon undertook the drafting of laws. Those Athenians who were in possession of a sizeable property and could provide their own weaponry had the right to participate in the city's administration. Of these, the *boule* or Council of Four Hundred and One was drawn by lot, with responsibilities of governance, while the Council of the *Areios Pagos* supervised observance of the laws and control of the archons.

Lending with the body as collateral continued to hold sway, the many were slaves of the few and power was in the hands of the latter. The people rebelled against the few and the conflict was serious. Both sides chose Solon as conciliator and *archon* (594 BC). He liberated the *demos*, prohibited lending, wrote off the debts private and public of the many and abolished the laws of Drakon, excepting those on homicide. He adopted new laws, which were written down and set up in the Royal (*Basileios*) Stoa. The Athenians were divided according to income (*pentakosiomedimnoi* = large landowners, *hippeis* = horsemen/"knights", *zeugitai* = ox-drivers). Citizens of the first two estates were entitled to participate in the city's administration as well as to assume correspondingly major or minor offices, whereas citizens of lower income had the right only of participation in the *ekklesia* of the *demos* (citizens' assembly) and in the law courts. The *boule* was made up of four hundred citizens, one hundred from each of the four tribes, and it entrusted the council of the Areios Pagos with implementation of the laws.

With Solon's departure from Athens, in order to avoid the pressures exerted on him to change one or other ordinance, new clashes broke out between the citizens. Three political factions were formed, the men of the plains (*pediakoi*) who were supporters of the oligarchy, the men of the coast (*paraloi*) who were supporters of the middle form of constitution (*mese politeia*), and the men of the hills (*diakrioi*) whose leader was Peisistratos, at that time advocate of the most democratic measures.

Possibly in 546/5 BC, Peisistratos succeeded in taking power for a third time and installed a tyranny, which not only lasted until his death (528/7 BC) but was also continued by his sons, until 511/0 BC. Peisistratos was mild and just in his governance of the city, employing political rather than tyrannical means. However, although he governed according to the laws, he took pains to ensure that members of his family assumed the principal offices [figs 26, 27]. He took particular care of the indigent farmers, granting them land and monetary loans, and setting up a body of judges who went into the countryside and resolved *in situ* differences between citizens. The intensive cultivation of the land increased the city's income, because Peisistratos imposed on farmers the payment of a tithe (one-tenth) of their yields. The concurrent development of craft-industry and trade brought a heyday for Athens. This prosperity is reflected in the projects on the Acropolis, as well the start of building works on the temple of Zeus Olympios and of Apollo Pythios in the same area, the Peisistrateian aqueduct and the construction of the Enneakrounos fountain, to channel water from the Kallirrhoe Spring on the banks of the River Ilissos. The private *ex-votos* too, mainly of korai statues on the Acropolis [figs 65, 98] and in other Attic sanctuaries, and the luxurious funerary monuments throughout Attica, which included statues of kouroi and korai [figs 30, 31, 64, 97], bear witness to the city's zenith.

The accidental assassination of Hipparchos (514 BC) — the target being his elder brother Hippias — by Harmodios and Aristogeiton, "for an affront in love" (Thucydides 6.59.1), was the beginning of the end of the tyranny. After his brother's death, Hippias governed so ruthlessly that the Alkmeonides, expressing the Athenians' sentiments, expelled him with Lacedaemonian assistance (511/0 BC). The city owed its liberation primarily to Sparta, but the democratic sentiment of the Athenians attributed it to Harmodios and Aristogeiton, whom they honoured posthumously, shortly after the expulsion of the tyrants, as tyrannicides [figs 23, 28].

In 508/7 BC the Alkmeonid Kleisthenes dominated the political scene of Athens and instituted political reforms that led to the founding of the Athenian democracy.

The reforms were underpinned by the creation of ten tribes, instead of the earlier four Ionian ones, which were based on phratries and clans, that is on the blood ties of their members. All the Athenians were incorporated in the ten tribes. The three regions of Attica, the plain, the interior and the coast, where citizens of different economic and social status lived, were represented equally in each tribe. So, Kleisthenes distributed the land of Attica into thirty local units, the *trittyes*, and each tribe consisted of three *trittyes*, one for each region. Each *trittyes* included a certain number of *demoi*. This reform achieved the best possible balanced social stratifi-

28 Athens, Ancient Agora. Part of the inscribed base of the statues of Harmodios and Aristogeiton. The epigram was known from the ancient sources. Shortly after the expulsion of the tyrants the Athenians set up a bronze statue group of the tyrannicides, a work of the sculptor Antenor, in 510 or 509 BC. Xerxes took the work as booty, when he captured the city in 480 BC. When the Persian Wars were over, the sculptors Kritios and Nesiotes created a new statue group, to the base of which this surviving part most probably belonged. Athens, Museum of the Ancient Agora.

28

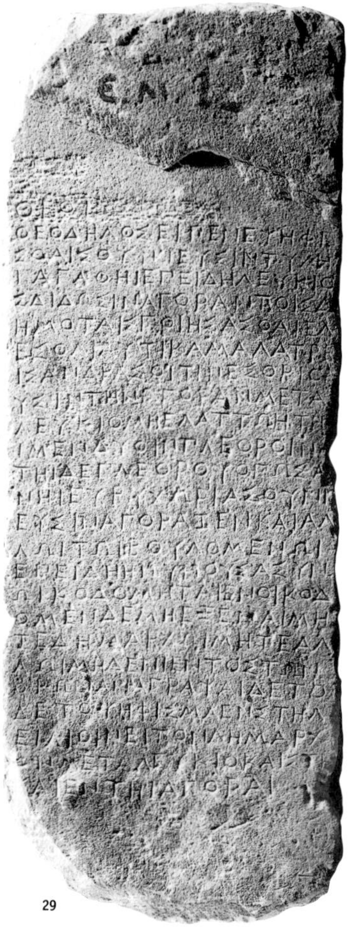

29

29 Decree of the demos of Sounieis, of the mid-4th century BC, in honour of Leukios. Their fellow citizen offered a plot of land for the building of a new agora of the demos, because the existing one had been encroached on by illegal buildings. According to the decree, no one, not even the demarchos, was allowed to build anything inside the limits of the new agora, the dimensions of which were 60 x 30 m. Trespassing on public land, even by those in public office, is not a phenomenon of modern times. Athens, Epigraphical Museum.

cation of the Athenians in the tribes, and the old political collectivities based on place of origin the city, the interior and the coast ceased to exist. The names of the settlements scattered throughout Attica were sometimes taken from the predominant clan thereabouts, e.g. Boutadai; sometimes from a distinctive feature of the place, e.g. the buckthorn (Gr. *rhamnos*) Rhamnous, the leek (Gr. *prason*) Prasiai; sometimes derived from a toponym, Phaleron-Phalereis, Sounion-Sounieis, Kephale-Kephalethen. With Kleisthenes' reforms they continued to keep their old names, now as *demoi*, while new *demoi* were also constituted. The number of *demoi* of Athens in Classical times, verified by inscriptions and literary texts, is about 140. The inhabitants of the *demoi*, the *demotai*, were entered in the registry of the *demos* to which they and their descendants were to belong, irrespective of their place of residence in the future. The Kleisthenian *demoi* were local autonomous organizations with their own elected authorities headed by the *demarchos*, their own *ekklesia* of the *demotai* and their own resources. They made decisions (decrees: fig. 29) relating to their local society, the incomes of the *demos*, the land, demotic and sacred, the local cults and their sanctuaries.

All ten Kleisthenian tribes were collective bodies but they were not local in character. The members of each tribe, *hoi phyletai*, made decisions on issues concerning their tribe, mainly relating to worship but also others, concerning the tribe's landholdings, its participation in the games, the age-sets of the ephebes, and so on. The army too, as reorganized by Kleisthenes, was tribally based. Each of the ten tribes provided one contingent of infantrymen (*hoplitai*) and one of horsemen (*hippeis*). Command of the army was entrusted to ten generals (*strategoi*) elected by the *demos*, one from each tribe. Over time, the office of *strategos* became the most important of the democracy.

The constitution of the Council of Five Hundred was also based on the ten tribes, consisting of fifty members (*bouleutai*) from each tribe. The *boule* exercised administrative power and part of the legal authority. However, it had first and foremost deliberative responsibilities. The issues dealt with by the *ekklesia* of the *demos* laws, decrees and all manner of other decisions taken by it were discussed beforehand in the *boule*, which submitted its recommendation on these, a preliminary decree (*probouleuma*), to the *demos*. Even so, because it was not easy for a body of five hundred men to discharge its daily administrative duties, the *boule* was divided into ten *prytaneiai*; each *prytaneia* consisted of the fifty *bouleutai* from each tribe and was responsible for the administration for one-tenth of the year. The *prytaneis* too convened the plenum of the *boule*, as well as the *ekklesia* of the *demos*.

The *ekklesia* of the *demos* met in regular and emergency sessions, in which all adult Athenian citizens participated. It was the principal instrument of

30

31

30, 31 Merenda. The tomb statue of Phrasikleia was found in 1972, carefully buried together with a kouros, at Merenda, the ancient demos of Myrrhinous. A work by the gifted sculptor of the Archaic period, Aristion from Paros, it preserves its original coloration in good condition. The name of the dead female is known from the epigram inscribed on the base of the statue, which had already been found in the 19th century, built into the wall of a church in Merenda. The letters had been deliberately damaged by hammering in recent times but the following text can be discerned (English rendering): "I am the monument of Phrasikleia. I shall always be called kore [maiden], because instead of marriage the gods endowed me with this name". Athens, National Archaeological Museum.

the Athenian democracy and wielded supreme legislative power, voting on laws and decrees, deciding on war or peace, and electing the archons.

Kleisthenes' reforms were of capital importance for the development of the Athenian democracy, which reached its fulfillment in the mid-fifth century BC with the reforms first of Ephialtes and then of Pericles. The democracy and the victory in the Persian Wars, to which the contribution of the democracy was paramount, led to the city's floruit in the fifth century BC.

Athens, like every city-state in Antiquity, was a community of citizens who were by origin Athenians, from both parents after the relevant law of Pericles. Adult male Athenian citizens participated in the government of the city, whereas females played no part in public life. The Athenian male was considered a citizen at the age of 18. Between the years of 18 and 20 he was incorporated in the age-set of the ephebes and was given military training, but also came into contact with politics and public life in general.

The outcome of the Persian Wars was decided by two battles on land, the battles of Marathon and Plataiai, and two battles at sea, of Salamis and Mykale. The battle of Marathon (490 BC) was *par excellence* an Athenian success, of which they were justly proud. Their victory was commemorated by the founding of a stone trophy on the battlefield, in the plain of Marathon, parts of which still survive [fig. 32]. The Athenians who fell in the battle were buried on the field because their virtue and valour were considered exceptional, as Thucydides writes (2.34.5) at the beginning of the funeral oration [figs 33, 34].

After the victory in the naval battle of Salamis (480 BC) and the repulsion of the Persian threat, Themistocles, to whose genius the triumph was largely

32 The "trophy" of Marathon crowned by a statue of Nike (Victory). A monument for the Victory was erected several years after the battle at the point of the Persians' final defeat. Two drums of the column and its capital are exhibited in the Archaeological Museum of Marathon.

33

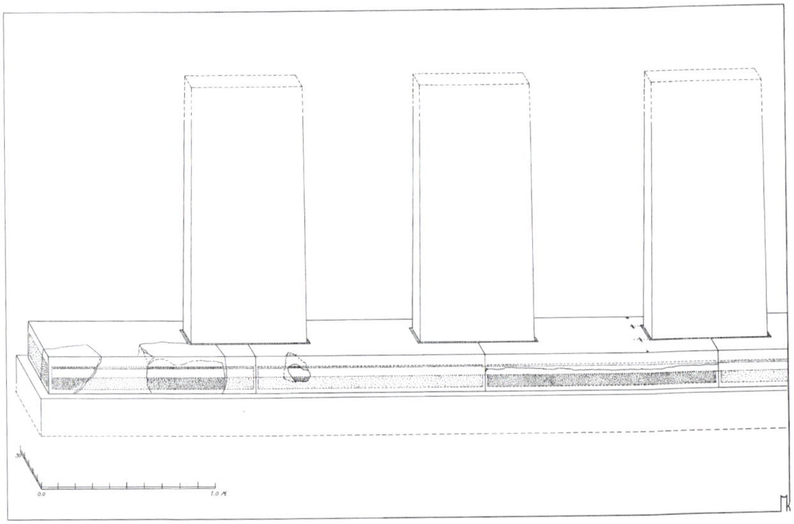

due, also proposed the fortification of the city [fig. 66], which was constructed not withstanding the Spartans' objections. The wall, which in fact enclosed a larger area than the existing city, was built very quickly, using material from the destroyed city, even from funerary monuments in the Kerameikos. Themistocles further proposed the fortifying and the building of the Piraeus, the urban plan of which conforms to the Hippodamean system. However, despite his contribution to the victories, to the recovery and the reinforcement of Athens, not even Themistocles escaped ostracism [fig. 35].

In 478 BC the First Athenian League was formed, an alliance intended to protect the Greek cities, and indeed those of Ionia, from the Persian menace. The Athenians decided which cities would contribute monies and which ships, and commissioned Aristeides "the Just" to define the sum of tribute each city should pay annually. The total tribute was set at 460 talents and the treasury of the League was on Delos. Kimon's victories over the Persians on land and sea, the gradual resignation of several allied cities from the commitment to provide ships, opting to pay tribute instead, the revolt of a few of the Athenians' allies (Naxos, Thasos), the transfer of the League treasury from Delos to the Acropolis (454/3 BC), the building of the Long Walls and the growing power of Athens led gradually to the transformation of the League into an Athenian hegemony. The Athenians adopted a harsh stance towards disobedient allies; the confrontation of the revolt of Euboea (445 BC) and the war against Samos (440–439 BC), in both operations the general in command was the *Olympian* Pericles, are telling examples.

Pericles, relying on the wealth and power of Athens, as well as on the allies' tribute money, conceived an ambitious building programme. A large part of the city and particularly the temples and the public buildings had been destroyed by the Persians, and there was now the possibility of erecting new edifices that would reflect the might of Athens [figs 67, 73]. Within an interval of some twenty years, the Parthenon [figs 36, 90], the Propylaia, the temples of Hephaistos [fig. 76], of the Ilissos, of Ares, of Sounion [figs 112, 144], the Telesterion of Eleusis [fig. 127] and several other public buildings were constructed.

Athens' heyday and excessive might overturned the balance of power, and forced Sparta to wage war upon her. The Athenians' involvement in the conflict between Corcyra (pres. Corfu) and Corinth over Epidamnos, an old colony of the latter in the Ionian Sea, the invasion of the Thebans into

33, 34 An incomplete stele with the names of Athenians belonging to the Erechtheis tribe who fell in the battle of Marathon, perhaps survives from the funerary monument of the Marathonomachoi, which until Pausanias' day still stood on the plain of Marathon. The Athenian ephebes honoured the dead by offering libations on the monument and holding games. They also held the funerary games in their memory, in front of the polyandrion, the cenotaph of the Marathonomachoi, which had been founded straight after the Persian Wars in the asty, in the official cemetery (Demosion Sema), outside the gates of the Kerameikos. The monument consisted of stelai standing a long base, on which were inscribed the names of the dead Athenians. Represented here is one member of the surviving part of the long base, on which epigrams in honour of the dead were inscribed, as well as the reconstruction drawing of the monument (by architect M. Korres). Athens, Ephorate of Prehistoric and Classical Antiquities of Attica.

34

Plataiai, ally of Athens, the revolt of Poteidaia, colony of Corinth, from the Athenian League, and the Athenians' decree excluding Megarians from Athenian harbours and markets, were the causes of the Peloponnesian War (431–404 BC). With the declaration of war, the Athenians living in *demoi* in the Attic countryside were forced to move with their families and chattels to the city, in order to escape the predations of the Peloponnesians, who invaded Attica from the very first year and every year after for the duration of hostilities. Many Athenians who, despite the synoecism and Kleisthenes' reforms, continued to live in the fields, moved to the *asty* with a heavy heart. They had great difficulty abandoning the places in which they had dwelt since time immemorial and, moreover, changing their way of life; as Thucydides remarks, they felt nothing less than each was deserting his city.

The number of adult Athenian citizens in 431 BC is estimated at around 60,000. The non-Athenians or metics were about 10,000 to 15,000. These were free men of foreign origin who lived permanently or for long intervals in the city, were obliged to pay taxes and to serve in the army. The number of slaves, most of whom were not Greeks, is very difficult to estimate and was possibly as high as 100,000. Some belonged to the city (*demosioi* = public) and were used in the administration, while the others belonged to private citizens and worked on the land, in the craft industries, in the mines and in the homes. Slave labour underpinned to a large degree the economy of the citizens; although not all and at the same time gave the Athenians more free time to spend on involvement in public affairs [figs 37, 38]. However, the poorer Athenians either had no slaves or, if they did, they worked with them on the land or in their small businesses. The total population of Attica on the outbreak of the Peloponnesian War was of the order of 300,000 to 400,000 persons.

The Athenians responded to the Peloponnesians' invasions with maritime raids on the coast of the Peloponnese, with incursions into Megara and with operations in West and Central Greece. The plague epidemic that struck first the Piraeus and then the city of Athens itself caused the death of many Athenians, among them Pericles and his two sons (429 BC). The principal

35a

35b

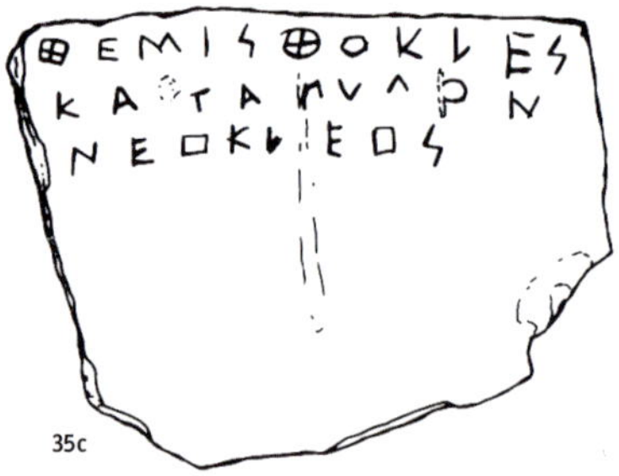

35c

35 Athens. Ostracism (488/7–417 BC) was directed initially against those Athenians who were friends of the tyrants, and subsequently against any powerful politician whose ambitions posed a threat to the democracy. For the process to be valid, a quorum of at least 6,000 citizens was required. Each Athenian wrote on a potsherd (ostrakon) the name of any fellow citizen he wanted banished. The person whose name appeared on the greatest number of sherds was ostracised for ten years. Written on the sherds is the name, frequently the patronymic or (and) the demotic of the candidate. Sometimes there were also insulting or sarcastic phrases against him (gossipy ostraka).

a On the first sherd Megakles, a powerful political figure in Athens, is deprecated as an adulterer. Megakles had not long returned after ten years in exile from his first ostracism, yet many citizens considered him a threat and voted again for his ostracism, in 472/1 BC.

b The citizen who wrote on the second sherd not only demanded the banishment of the famous general Kimon, but also that he take with him his sister Elpinike, well known for her dynamism and meddling in public affairs. The sherd dates from the ostracism of 472/1 BC.

c The third sherd is directed against Themistocles and also belongs to the ostracism of 472/1 BC. He was in fact ostracised one year later. The sherd is one of the very many (2,175) that have been found inscribed with his name. Not even Themistocles escaped denigration; the Athenian who incised the sherd calls him "katapygon" (= given to unnatural lust). Athens, Kerameikos Museum.

new statesman who came to the fore after Pericles was Kleon, who advocated a more aggressive policy against the Spartans. The cruel and violent subjugation of Lesbos, which had revolted from the Athenian League, the events in Pylos, which ended in captivity for the beleaguered Lacedaemonians, the devastating defeat of the Athenians at Delion in Boeotia (424 BC), their refusal to accept the peace proposals of Sparta, the expedition to and siege of Amphipolis, where Kleon was killed, were the main events in this turbulent period.

Kleon led the Athenians in a more intransigent stance towards their allies, as borne out *inter alia* by an Attic decree, of which only a few fragments have survived, imposing the use of Attic coinage, measurements and weights on them. A second decree, also in fragmentary condition, reassesses the amount of annual tribute levied on the allies. Through these measures, Kleon's administration endeavoured to increase the city's income, in order to meet the growing needs of the war.

With the death of Kleon and of his adversary, the Lacedaemonian Brasidas, in Amphipolis, more moderate opinions prevailed and the two cities contracted the Nikian Peace (421–415 BC), thus named after its prime mover, the Athenian general Nikias. But the peace did not prevent some clashes and the Athenians imposed the harshest of punishments on the initially neutral island of Melos, which refused to surrender (416/5 BC). The moderate Nikias now dominated the political scene, while Alcibiades had already made his entry. The Sicilian Expedition (415–413 BC), the Athenians' attempt to extend their domination to the West, an idea that Alcibiades passionately supported, and the ignominious defeat they suffered, were decisive for the outcome of the war. The Peloponnesians then circumvallated Dekeleia and transferred hostilities to the heart of Attica. They also successfully sought an alliance with Persia, which together with the Athenians' defeat in Sicily incited the revolt of most of the Ionian cities, with first and foremost Chios. Alcibiades' triumphs in the area of the Hellespont and the Athenians' victory at Arginousai were not sufficient to turn the tide. Their crushing defeat at Aigos Potamoi led to the blockade of Athens and its acceptance of the humiliating terms of the peace. The democracy was overthrown, and with the Lacedaemonians' support the repressive regime of the Thirty Tyrants was installed (summer 404–September 403 BC). Their policy was violent and corrupt, and they assassinated many citizens and confiscated their property. A few democratic fugitives who had sought refuge in Thebes, headed by Thrasyboulos, captured the fort of Phyle [fig. 39] on Mount Parnes, from which they launched raids against the tyrants. Boosted by their successes, they went on to capture Mounichia in the Piraeus. The forays intensified and the oligarchs requested help from the Lacedaemonians. Lysander and King Pausanias sped to their aid with troops, but the latter turned indirectly

36

36 Athens. The Parthenon was built between 447/6 and 433/2 BC. The annual authority of the epistatai (overseers) of the project had the yearly accounts inscribed on a stele of Pentelic marble, which was set up on the Acropolis. In the account shown here, for 434/3 BC, stated immediately after the reference to the date (of the building programme and the civil year) is the sum carried over from the previous year, which is followed by the sum made available by the tamiai (treasurers) of Athens in the current year and the sum of money from the sale of surplus gold and ivory. Next comes the expenditure on purchasing materials and for contracting, for the workmen at Pentele, as well as on transporting marble and on the remuneration of the sculptors who worked on the statues for the pediments. Athens, Epigraphical Museum.

37

37, 38 Athens. The Agora of Athens was the venue not only of many public functions of the city but also of marketing goods, practising trades (barbers, shoemakers, etc.), all manner of transactions and encounters of citizens. Life there, public and private, is known both from ancient authors and from excavations and their finds, among them inscriptions. Brief texts inscribed on sherds (fragments of broken vases) give us a vivid picture of everyday life. Of the two illustrated here, the first [fig. 37] is a message left by someone for a man named Thamneus, asking him to leave his saw under the threshold of the garden door. The second [fig. 38] is, according to the interpretation by Stephanos N. Koumanoudis, a "billet doux" from a youth named Arkesimos to his beloved Eumelis, asking her to meet him as soon as possible. Evidently his parents are away from home and he is burning with amorous passion. Athens, Museum of the Ancient Agora.

towards the democrats. With Lacedaemonian mediation both sides were reconciled, swore that they would bear no grudges and the democracy was restored. It was then that a significant change took place; on the proposal of the orator Archinos, one of the heroes of Phyle, who had assigned sovereignty to the *demos*, the *ekklesia* voted the official use of the Ionic alphabet instead of the old Attic one [fig. 40], thus setting the seal on the end of a process that had begun long before.

In the early fourth century BC Sparta tried to dominate Asia Minor and collided with Persia. In Greece itself, Persian-instigated opposition to the Spartan hegemony swelled, resulting in the outbreak of the so-called Corinthian War (395/4 BC).

In 394 BC the Lacedaemonians were vanquished by the Persian fleet, under the command of the Athenian Konon, in the naval battle of Knidos. Immediately after, Konon sailed to Athens and with the help of the crews and of some foreign cities, mainly Thebes, as well as with pecuniary funding partly from Persia, rebuilt the city's walls, which had been demolished at the end of the Peloponnesian War [figs 41, 42, 174]. The walls once again secured the liberty and autonomy of Athens against Sparta. The continuation of the Corinthian War, with fluctuating intensity, led Sparta to sue for peace, despite its successes. Many of its adversaries also desired cessation of hostilities. Persia, fomented by Sparta, seized the opportunity to directly intervene in Greek affairs. The Peace of Antalkidas (387/6 BC), named after the Spartan who had an important role in concluding the peace, imposed the Great King's will on the Greeks. The Greek cities of Asia Minor and Cyprus passed to his sovereignty, while he acknowledged the autonomy of the other Greek cities, large and small, and the right of the Athenians to the islands of Lemnos, Imbros and Skyros, which they had always possessed. The peace guaranteed the interests of Sparta and allowed it to interfere at will in order to impose the autonomy of the cities.

A few years later (378/7 BC), the Athenians reacted by founding the Second Athenian League. The new alliance was constituted by a decree of the city [fig. 43] and its declared aim was to rid the Greeks of Lacedaemonian hegemonic designs, whereas it concurrently recognized Persian sovereignty over the Greek cities of Asia Minor. It was purely defensive in character and, in contrast to the League of the fifth century BC, it safeguarded its members from the threat of turning into an Athenian hegemony by allowing each city its freedom, autonomy and body politic of its choice, and by prohibiting the installation of an Athenian garrison and archon. Participants in the League included several powerful cities, Chios, Mytilene, Methymna, Rhodes, cities of Euboea and of Thrace, Thebes, the

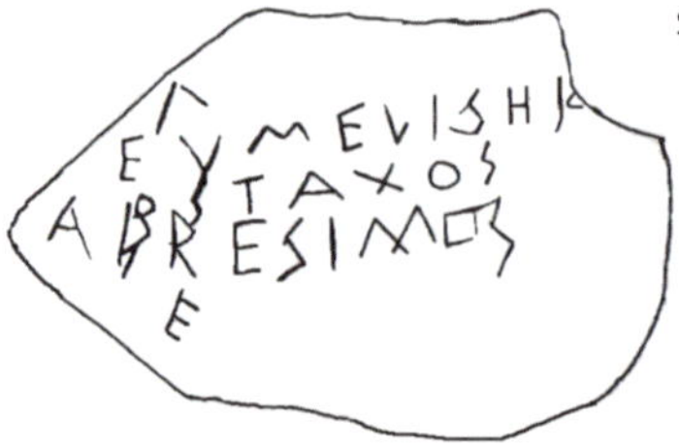

38

tyrant of Pherai Jason and the *Koinon* of Chalkideans. The Athenians' naval successes in the Aegean, against the Lacedaemonians, significantly increased the number of allies.

In the domestic sphere, the growth of Athenian trade and manufacturing, the systematic exploitation of the Laurion mines, based on slave labour, and the development of banking transactions, led to the accumulation of wealth, mainly in the hands of merchants. However, it also caused a turnabout in the citizens' attitude to the state and they came to construe their participation in public affairs according to the degree that the state served their interests. The monetary remuneration for attending sessions of the assembly of the *demos* (*ekklesiastikos misthos*), introduced at this time, clearly reflects this stance. Provision was made also for disbursing to citizens a share of the *"theorika"*, that is, the money originally given for them to attend theatrical performances.

The Athenian democracy continued to function without interruption. New politicians appeared on the scene, who contributed to shaping the foreign

39 Phyle. In 404/3 BC the fort of Phyle on Mount Parnes (near the village of Chasia) was captured by Thrasyboulos and some seventy other exiled Athenian democrats. Thrasyboulos and his companions used the fort as a launching pad for operations and were joined by other democratic Athenians who sped to join forces with them after their first successes, in order to overthrow the tyrannical regime of the Thirty. The walls in the photograph date from the early 4th century BC.

39

40 Athens. Part of an Attic decree (440–432 BC) making provisions for the smooth functioning of the public water conduits of the city. It also honours the sons of Pericles, Paralos and Xanthippos, for their services. The decree is inscribed in the Attic alphabet, in which the letter E renders the vowels ε (epsilon), η (eta) and frequently the spurious diphthong ει (epsilon-iota), while the letter O renders ο (omikron), ω (omega) and frequently the spurious diphthong ου (omicron-ypsilon). The letter H renders the aspirate, Λ renders γ (gamma), L = λ (lambda) and σ (sigma) has the form ≤ and later Σ, the letters XΣ and ΦΣ render respectively the consonant clusters ξ (xi) and ψ (psi). Athens, Epigraphical Museum.

and the domestic policy of the state. The most senior was Agyrrhios, followed by Kallistratos, Euboulos and Demosthenes. The city's military affairs were directed primarily by Timotheos, son of Konon, Iphikrates, Chabrias and Laches.

Two laws of this period shed light on the Athenians' position in critical internal sectors. The first law (375/4 BC) protected the genuine, after public assay, silver Attic coin [fig. 44] against the counterfeits that apparently circulated in large quantities on account of trade. The second (374/3 BC) was intended to secure sufficient supplies of wheat and barley from the islands of Lemnos, Imbros and Skyros, and their availability in the Athenian market when the need arose, at a price fixed by the *demos*. Attica did not enjoy autarky in cereal cultivation and was always obliged to import grain to meet its needs. This lack was a basic and diachronic problem, which came to a head when, for natural reasons or because of war, the harvest was poor either in Attica or in the regions from which Athens obtained grain, in Greece or abroad (Pontos, Egypt, Sicily).

During the years of the Theban hegemony (371–362 BC), Athens engaged in military operations in the northern and eastern Aegean, capturing Samos and installing cleruchs there, while in Andros and Amorgos, and possibly in other islands too, garrisons were installed, despite the declared principle of the Second Athenian League. Its attitude towards the allies provoked the revolt of the cities of Kea against it (363/2 BC) and later (357 BC) the revolt of its three powerful allies, Chios, Kos and Rhodes. In the same period, the new ascendant power of Macedonia, under the leadership of Philip II, was manifesting its expansionist designs by invading the Chalkidike. The growing might of the Macedonians and the military campaigns of Philip led to confrontation with Athens. In the battle of Chaironeia (338/7 BC) the Athenians were overwhelmingly defeated, losing 1,000 men, while 2,000 more were taken captive: extremely severe losses for a city whose population was no more than 30,000 adult males.

Even so, the defeat did not restrain the city's dynamism [fig. 47]. The Athenians took immediate measures to fortify their city, as is evidenced by the partially preserved decree (possibly of 338/7 BC) referring to the repair of the Long Walls and of the Piraeus. For the reconstruction material even private funerary monuments from the Kerameikos were used and the citizens gave of their personal labour.

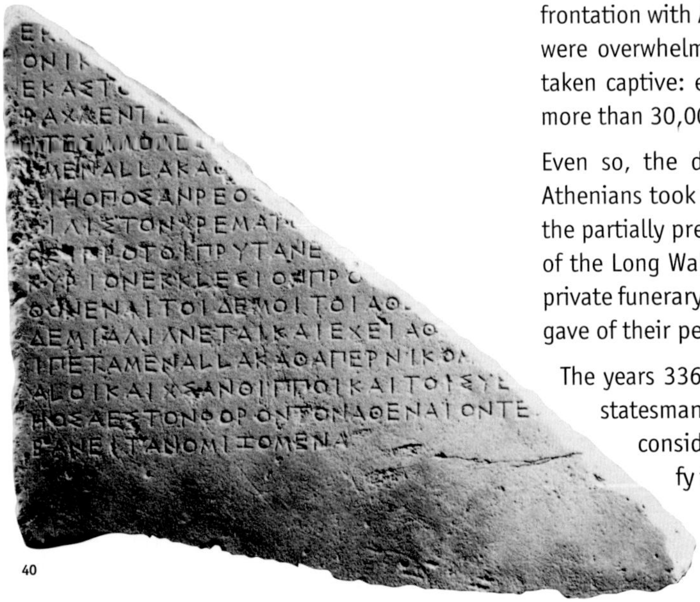

40

The years 336–324 BC are characterized by the activity of the orator and statesman, Lykourgos. In control of the state treasury, he succeeded in considerably increasing the annual income, which he used to fortify the city, to enlarge the shipyards, to build a fleet of four hundred trieremes, to reorganize the institution of Ephebeia and to implement a programme of public works rivalling that of Pericles. It was then that the Panathenaic Stadium was

41

41, 42 Piraeus. After their defeat in the Peloponnesian War (404 BC), the Athenians demolished large sections of the Long Walls and of the Piraeus, obeying the commands of the Lacedaemonians. The systematic rebuilding **[fig. 41**, part of the walls of the Piraeus] of the walls, after the defeat of the latter in the naval battle of Knidos (394 BC), is due to the Athenian Konon, then head of the Persian fleet. The fragmentary inscription **[fig. 42]** of 394/3 BC was found in Piraeus. Like others of its kind, it is an account for the costs of rebuilding part of the walls of the Piraeus. Athens, Epigraphical Museum.

built of stone [fig. 45], the Theatre of Dionysos was renovated [figs 73, 114] and buildings were constructed in the Lyceum (Lykeion) Gymnasium. Works were also carried out in the sanctuary of Demeter at Eleusis and of Amphiaraos at Oropos, where the festival and games in honour of the god, the Amphiaraia, were instituted. Lykourgos was also responsible for the official record of the plays by the three great tragic poets.

The death of Lykourgos (324 BC) and of Alexander the Great (323 BC) were pivotal events in the history of Athens [fig. 46]. By joining forces with other cities which sought to put an end to Macedonian domination, it became embroiled in the Lamian War. Its terrible defeat in 322 BC had enduring consequences and it never recovered its status as paramount naval power. Athens lost Oropos and Samos, and, far worse, was forced to accept a Macedonian garrison in the Piraeus. The orators Demosthenes, Hypereides and Eukrates were put on trial as opponents of the Macedonians and were condemned to death. Athens passed to direct Macedonian control and Kassander appointed as head of the city Demetrios Phalereus (317–307/6 BC). His governance was mild, but the regime became oligarchic and the terms of Athenian citizenship were redefined, while democratic institutions encumbering the wealthy classes, such as sponsorship of theatrical performances (*choregia*), remuneration of citizens for attending sessions of the public assembly (*ekklesiastikos misthos*) and recompense of citizens for attending theatrical performances (*theorika*) were abolished [fig. 48]. Demetrios Phalereus was ousted by Demetrios Poliorketes, who also declared the city's independence. The democratic regime was reinstated and the supporters of Phalereus were sent into exile.

42

43 Athens. The illustrated decree (378/7 BC) is the prospectus of the Second Athenian League, accompanied by a list of the allied cities. The alliance was intended to rid Hellas of the hegemonic sights of the Lacedaemonians. There were two contributing members, the Athenians and their allies. The alliance was directed by the ekklesia of the demos and the synhedrion (joint assembly) of the allies, which met in Athens but without the participation of the Athenians. Every decision had to be approved by both bodies. Athens, Epigraphical Museum.

43

The principal source of knowledge of Athenian history in the ensuing centuries are the abundant, but frequently fragmentary inscriptions, since long texts by ancient authors like those of the fifth and fourth centuries BC do not exist. Because of the gaps in the sources and their piecemeal nature, it is impossible to compose a complete and continuous history of Athens from the death of Alexander the Great until early imperial times, and even more so of the years after.

From the third century BC onwards, Athens no longer played a leading role in Greek affairs and its fortunes depended on the powers of the day, initially of Macedonia and subsequently of Rome. Foreign policy was dictated by its relations with these powers. Analogous was its position, usually opportunistic, vis-à-vis the other kingdoms of Alexander's successors (*Diadochoi*) and the provincial powers (Aetolia, Rhodes, et al.).

In 287 BC Athens expelled the Macedonian garrison from the hill of the Mouseion and cast off the Macedonian yoke. For twenty-seven years (287–262 BC) it remained independent. In 268/7 BC it joined a coalition of forces, in which Sparta under Areas I and Egypt under Ptolemy II were the most powerful, against Macedonian domination. During hostilities, the Ptolemaic presence on the side of Athens was strong. Ptolemy's admiral Patroklos installed two bases in Attica, the first on Gaidouronisi off Cape Sounion, referred to by Pausanias as "Patroclus' island", and the second the army camp at Kotroni near Porto Rafti, as confirmed by excavations and particularly the numerous coins of Ptolemy II found there. However, Ptolemy's assistance did not avert defeat. The negative outcome (262 BC) of the so-called Chremonidean War put Athens under the Macedonian yoke of Antigonos Gonatas once again. A garrison was installed again on the hill of the Museion and the Macedonians took control of the Attic forts. The city's foreign policy was now dictated by Antigonos. The *ekklesia* of the *demos* was concerned only with domestic issues and indeed, as the surviving decrees show, of secondary importance. The instruments of the democratic body politic, the *ekklesia* of the *demos*, the *boule* and the various archons, continued to exist, but their powers were curtailed and the eponymous archons were no longer selected by drawing lots but were elected from among socially eminent men. The number of ephebes was drastically reduced, as was the number of cavalrymen-*hippeis* [fig. 49].

After the death of Antigonos Gonatas (239 BC) and the accession of his son Demetrios II to the throne of Macedonia, Athens took part in the so-called Demetrian War, waged by the monarch against the Aetolians and the Achaeans, until his death (229 BC). The arena of war was frequently shifted to Attica, even to the Academy, destroying the crops. Demetrios' death meant the liberation of Athens. The Piraeus, Salamis and the garrison in

44 Athens. Attic silver coin of the 4th century BC. The head of Athena and the owl, emblem of the city of Athens, were standard and unchanging subjects on the city's coinage from Archaic times into the Roman period. Athens, Museum of the Ancient Agora.

45 Athens. The Panathenaic Stadium (330/29 BC) in its full form and built of stone was one of the major public works attended to by the statesman and orator Lykourgos. It was used for the foot races in the games held on the occasion of the Panathenaia festival. The stadium was rebuilt (between AD 139/40 and 143/4) at the expenses of the fabulously wealthy Athenian Herodes Atticus. It owes its present aspect to extensive restoration and reconstruction in 1896, for it to host the first modern Olympic Games.

44

45

46

46 Athens. The name Lykophron son of Lykourgos from the *demos* of Boutadai, inscribed on the fragmentary grave stele, is of the father of the renowned orator and statesman Lykourgos (*ca* 390–324 BC), while the preserved ending of a female name that follows very probably belongs to his mother. The stele was found in 1979, together with two other inscribed funerary monuments of relatives of Lykourgos, in the excavation of tombs of the 5th and 4th centuries BC, adjacent to Plato's Academy (Akademia Platonos). It emerges from the inscriptions that the family tomb (erion) of the orator stood there. Athens, Ephorate of Prehistoric and Classical Antiquities of Attica.

47 Athens. The illustrated law (337/6 BC) was found in the ancient Agora. It was passed shortly after the Athenians' crushing defeat by Philip II of Macedon at Chaironeia in Boeotia (338 BC). Its purpose was to protect institutionally democracy from a possible coup due to Macedonian rule, which was spreading over Greece, and the burgeoning of pro-Macedonian tendencies in Athens. The demos was afraid that the bouleutai of the Areios Pagos, vestige of the aristocratic regime, would not remain loyal to the democracy. The law repeats the earlier anti-tyrannical legislation, foreseeing pardon for the assassin of a person who attempted to dissolve the demos or the democracy. However, its principal concern was to put obstacles in the way of the possible participation of members of the Areios Pagos in a session of the body, if the democracy was abolished. Above the inscription there is a relief, the subject of which appears to be Demokratia crowning with a wreath the Demos of the Athenians. Athens, Museum of the Ancient Agora.

Mounichia and Rhamnous passed once again into Athenian hands. Protagonists in the liberation were the brothers Eurykleides and Mikion from the *demos* of Kifissia, but the head of the Achaean Confederacy, Aratos, also played a decisive role. Despite his hopes, the Athenians did not join the Confederacy, opting for neutrality and refusing to come to its aid when requested (225 BC), in order to confront Kleomenes of Sparta.

On their liberation, the Athenians tried to erase from their public events and decrees all mention of the Macedonian kings and their family. The Macedonian bronze coins in use were melted down and recast with Athenian symbols. The Athenians drew up plans to strengthen the walls, the Piraeus and the defence of the forts. It seems that a decision was taken not to repair the Long Walls, as is deduced from Polybius' testimony that it was preferable and less expensive to fortify Athens and the Piraeus separately. It is illuminating that from the third century BC onwards the decrees refer to the *Asty* and the Piraeus as two cities.

In the last thirty years of the third century BC three wars were waged, the third of which is known to history as the First Macedonian War (215–205 BC) and was the pretext for Rome's involvement for the first time in Greek affairs. It sided with the Aetolians and Attalos I of Pergamon (241–197 BC) against Macedonia and the Achaian Confederacy. For as long as Eurykleides and Mikion held the reins of power in Athens they strove to cultivate amicable relations with all the other cities, and so Athens did not take part in any of the three wars. However, it appears that its economic situation was far from good and it is indicative that the number of ephebes, 20–55 per annum, is small too, as surmised from ephebic decrees of the last quarter of the century.

The Athenians were unable to cope with circumstances and the Macedonians invaded Attica, advancing as far as the Academy. The dual attack by Philip V and his general Philokles on Athens and the Piraeus brought in its wake looting of the unprotected countryside, rural sanctuaries and temples. When the war ended, after the decisive defeat of the Macedonians by the Roman consul Titus Flamininus, in the battle of Kynos Kephalai (Cynoscephalae) in 197 BC, and the negotiations for the peace treaty, the Athenians made no territorial gains.

On the outbreak of the Third Macedonian War (171–168 BC), that is, the clash between the Romans and the Macedonians under King Perseus, the Athenians offered to help the Romans by dispatching troops and ships. Rome declined the offer and instead requested large quantities of grain for its armies. Despite the persistent problem of insufficient grain supplies faced by the city, it took measures to supply the Romans with the amounts required. The war ended with Perseus' defeat at Pydna (168 BC) and the

Athenians, enjoying the favour of the Senate, succeeded in securing the islands of Delos and Lemnos, and most probably Imbros and Skyros.

The long period of peace experienced by the city of Athens, it was involved in a war only in 88 BC, the acquisition of Delos and Lemnos, and the already existing ties with the strong powers of the time, Egypt and the kingdom of the Seleucids and of the Attalids, brought stability and an economic upturn. To the latter contributed the issue, possibly from 164 BC, of the "New Style" Attic silver coins [fig. 50], minting of which ceased, most probably, in the decade 50–40 BC.

Athens' close relations with Egypt are reflected in the victories in the Panathenaic Games, of kings Ptolemy V and Ptolemy VI, and members of the royal family, between 182 and 158 BC.

Works on completing the temple of Zeus Olympios in Athens [figs 45, 56], with a donation from the Seleucid king Antiochos IV Epiphanes (175–164 BC), the construction of the Stoa of Eumenes next to the Theatre of Dionysos [fig. 73], gift of King Eumenes II of Pergamon (197–159 BC), and the two-storey stoa in the Agora [fig. 78] built by his brother Attalos II Philadelphos (159–138 BC), are incontrovertible proof that, in contrast to the preceding centuries, major building projects were no longer financed by the city, as in the past, but by foreign rulers. Thus, these potentates displayed not only their admiration for Athens but also their wealth and power.

Glimpses into aspects of Athenian society in the period are offered by two of of the city's festivals, for which abundant epigraphic testimonies survive, the Panathenaia and the Theseia. Both were celebrated every fourth year. The inscriptions yield information on athletics and equestrian games, in which not only Athenian citizens took part, but also foreigners; and indeed in the equestrian contests it was often kings and princes, Ptolemies, Seleucids and Attalids, who competed, not in person but with their horses and chariots, as well as with jockeys and charioteers who raced in their name. In the games of the Theseia, a festival in honour of the founder-hero (*oikistes*) of Athens, Theseus, mainly Athenians took part, except in two team contests, of "*euandria*" (physical fitness) and of "*euoplia*" (good state of arms and equipment), in which foreigners were allowed to compete, provided they were mercenaries and resident in Athens.

Whereas the inscriptions pertaining to the two festivals give a picture of a vital and vigorous society, the ephebic inscriptions of the closing years of the third and the first three decades of the second century BC reveal another side. From the end of the fourth century BC the Ephebeia was no longer of two year duration, but one year, and the enrolment of the ephebes had ceased to be compulsory. Because the state did not provide weapons for the ephebes, only youths from affluent families registered. So, their number fell

47

appreciably, ranging between 20 and 50 each year. The number rose after 167 BC, when the economic situation started to improve, but did not exceed 200. As Ch. Habicht points out, the training of this small "select" band of ephebes was intended to prepare the future leaders of the city, in the army and the navy, in politics and administration, inculcating through instruction democratic values and patriotic virtues.

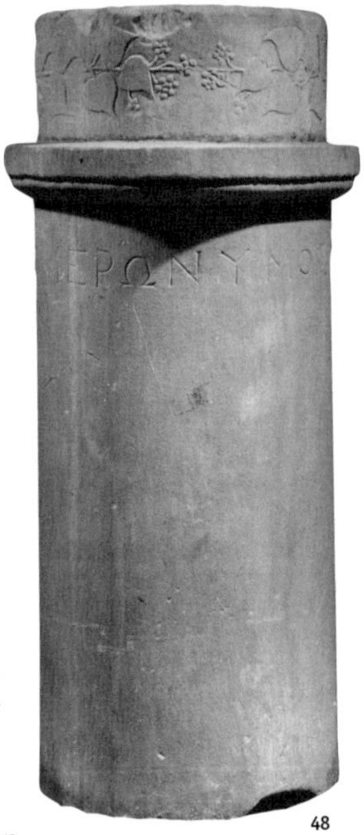

48

48 Athens. Demetrios Phalereus enacted a law drastically curtailing the expenses and luxury of ceremonies for the dead and of funerary monuments. Production of lavish and artistic grave reliefs ceased, and their place was taken by plain oblong stelai, tables and columnar monuments (kioniskoi) crowned with a ring. These kinds of funerary monuments prevailed in the ensuing centuries. Athens, Epigraphical Museum.

The sack of Corinth (146 BC) by the Romans, after the defeat of the Achaean Confederacy, gave new impetus to the development of Delos, which the Romans had ceded to Athens in 167 BC. Maritime trade was now conducted mainly through Delos, because it was a free port, and the island attained its zenith in the last quarter of the second century BC. A consequence of this was the economic boom and prosperity of Athens. New families appeared in the city, whose wealth and power was based on trade and their relations with Delos. Members of these families assumed the highest political offices. The economic boom led to the significant increase, in relation to previous years, in the annual number of ephebes, and around 120 BC the first ephebes of foreign origin appear. Their presence is due too to the city's long and undiminished fame as a centre of high-quality education. The philosophical schools, the Academy, the Stoa and the Garden (*Kepos*) of Epikouros were all flourishing and attracted foreign students in great number. Moreover, the ephebes were obliged to attend lessons in philosophy, as attested by decrees of the period, in which they are praised because during their service they regularly attended all the classes provided in the gymnasia, the Academy, the Lyceum [fig. 133] and the Ptolemaion.

The thriving economy, the accumulation of wealth in the hands of a few and the harsh working conditions for a large part of the populace led to two

49

49 Athens. This lead tablet is one of the one hundred and more found in an ancient well in the Agora and originating from the archive of the cavalry. Many others had been found earlier in the Kerameikos. The tablets date from the 4th to the 3rd century BC. Written on one side is the name of the horseman and on the other is frequently his name again, the colour of his horse (white, brown, black, etc.), the symbol (axe, lightning flash, trident, etc.) with which it was branded, and the value of the steed. Each cavalryman kept on his person an exact copy of the tablet. If the horse was killed in battle, the horseman or his family — if he too were slain — received the specified compensation. Athens, Museum of the Ancient Agora.

50 Athens. The "New Style" silver coins minted by the city of Athens (*ca* 164/3–perhaps 54/3 BC) carry on the obverse the head of Athena with helmet, and on the reverse some standard features, amphora and owl, symbols of the city, and the initials ΑΘΕ(ναίον), and some which changed annually or even monthly. The names (originally monograms and later abbreviated) of the two annual archons responsible for the mint also appear. In 136/5 BC and for some fifty years after, the name of a third archon was added, which changed each month. All the elements on the reverse were enclosed by an olive branch. Athens, Museum of the Ancient Agora.

50

51 Lavrion, Souriza. Water cistern of the "Asklepiakon" ore washery of the lessee-entrepreneur Simos from the *demos* of Paiania. For centuries the Laurion mines played an important role in underpinning the Athenian economy.

51

52

52 Athens. Regulations for the use of the Library of Pantainos, which was founded in the ancient Agora in the reign of Trajan (AD 98–117). "No book shall be taken out of the library, because we have sworn an oath. The Library shall be open from the 1st to the 6th hour". Athens, Museum of the Ancient Agora.

rebellions by slaves labouring in the Laurion mines [figs 51, 148]. Indeed, in the second rebellion, at the end of the century, they captured the fort of Sounion as well.

However, the outcome of the war also had a long-lasting negative effect on Athens. The Romans imposed their permanent presence in Macedonia and from there spread to large parts of Greece, among them regions neighbouring Attica: Megara, Thebes and Chalkis. They had come to Greece to stay.

The outbreak of war (89 BC) between the Romans and the king of Pontos Mithridates VI Eupator was a critical turning point for Athens' relations with Rome. For reasons that elude us, the Athenians sided with Mithridates. In March 86 BC, the Romans under Sulla broke through the city wall, between the Piraeus Gate and the Sacred Gate, and captured Athens. They then indulged in a frenzy of slaughter and pillage. Traces of the enormous destruction they caused have come to light in excavations in the Agora, the Asklepieion to the south of the Acropolis [fig. 116], and the Kerameikos. They stole the gold and silver treasures from the Acropolis, and transported many artworks to Rome. Delos did not escape the Romans' rage either, because during the war Mithridates' fleet had butchered Romans and Italiots on the island. The Athenians' defeat drew along with it the somewhat tyrannical regime of Aristion, who had succeeded the likewise "tyrannical" Athenion.

Sulla did not inflict any other punishment on the Athenians and in fact allowed them to keep Delos. However, the ravaging of Athens bought poverty and the city was obliged to borrow money from private individuals, among them foreigners. Romans who had a Greek education and who held Hellenic civilization in high regard, such as Cicero's friend Titus Pomponius, surnamed Atticus, offered money and grain. Twenty-five years were to pass before Athens was in a position to implement a programme of reconstructing public buildings. However, then too most of the money came from foreign rulers and Roman generals, such as Pompey and Caesar, and officials such as Appius Claudius Pulcher, who gifted money for the Lesser Propylaia of Eleusis [fig. 128]. The cost of rebuilding the Odeion of Pericles was met by Ariobarzanes II of Cappadocia, who like other rulers had been educated in Athens and is recorded among the ephebes in an ephebic list of 80/79 BC.

In the Roman Civil Wars, Athens haplessly sided successively with those who were defeated each time; first with Pompey against Caesar, then with Brutus against Mark Anthony and Octavian, and finally with Mark Anthony against Octavian. In all three cases the city escaped punishment, but any autonomy it still had was dealt a mortal blow. After the naval battle of Actium (31 BC), from which Octavian Augustus emerged as sole sovereign of the Roman Empire [fig. 53], Athens remained a self-governing city but became part of the imperial province of Achaea (27 BC et seq.). It lived on the fame of its past, while it was at the same time a notable centre of culture [figs 76, 81] to which foreigners came for longer or shorter sojourns [fig. 52]. The presence of Romans is attested from the early second century BC and became increasingly conspicuous over the years [fig. 82]. Some came for the philosophical schools, others as officials or merchants. Some who were powerful public figures at home came because they were sent into exile or to avoid exile. Some of the Romans domiciled permanently in Athens entered their sons in the sets of Athenian ephebes and on completion of their service these youths were entitled to become Athenian citizens. Ephebes of Roman origin do not appear in the ephebic lists earlier than the last quarter of the century. The same *terminus post quem* seems to apply to the holding of public offices by citizens of Roman origin, in the first century BC, sporadically in the first half of the century and more frequently in the second, according to the evidence of the inscriptions.

The Romans' admiration for Greek civilization and in particular for the city of Athens is epitomized and best expressed by the person of Emperor Hadrian (AD 117–138) [fig. 80]. During his reign new life was insufflated into Athens, after many years of neglect. He visited the city three times and during his

53 Athens, Acropolis. After the naval battle of Actium (31 BC) and his victory over Mark Anthony, Octavian (Augustus) took no reprisals against Athens, even though it had sided with his adversary. The Athenians set up portrait statues of him and of his wife Livia, and accorded him the appellations Soter (Saviour) and Euergetes (Benefactor). A few years later (post-27 BC), a small circular temple in honour of Augustus and the goddess Roma was built on the Acropolis.

53

54 Athens. This inscription is carved on the last step of a small staircase leading from the orchestra to the skene of the Theatre of Dionysos. From the form of the letters it is dated to the 4th/5th century AD. From the content it emerges that the dedicator, Phaidros son of Zoilos, held the office of eponymous archon of the city, although when exactly is not known. The construction of the bema of the theatre was not connected with the monument's original function, for dramatic performances, but with its use, attested from the 4th century BC, also as a venue for the ekklesia of the demos.

55 Athens. Funerary inscription of Christian times (5th/6th c. AD). Found near the church of the Holy Trinity in the Kerameikos. Agape was a Christian woman, as the three incised crosses indicate. Was she young? Athens, Epigraphical Museum.

54

55

stays he favoured it as none other. He expanded the city to the southwest, founding the "city of Hadrian" [figs 56, 90] as complement to the old "city of Theseus". He completed the temple of Zeus Olympios, built the Panhellenion, a temple dedicated to Zeus Panhellenios, a new pompeion (a building for the preparation of processions), a gymnasium and a stoa with library, and constructed an aqueduct. He planned the founding of the Panhellenion, a confederation of all the Greek-speaking cities, headed by Athens, where its representatives met annually. The emperor's more general social policy is reflected in two decisions that had beneficial consequences for the inhabitants of Athens, the law on the uncontrolled export of olive oil from Attica and the letter on the trade of fish. To these measures should be added the confiscation and distribution of the land property of the wealthy magnate Hipparchos, grandfather of Herodes Atticus.

In the reign of Marcus Aurelius (AD 161–180) the Romans' intellectual ties with the city of Athens were reinforced further, while the emperor himself, in a long letter (AD 174/5), judges the appeals to him on disputes between Athenians. One petition concerns the altercation between the Athenians and Herodes Atticus, whom they had accused of economic tyranny to their detriment. Herodes Atticus (AD 101–177) [fig. 79] encapsulates two principal traits of the period; the first is the prime importance of rhetoric as high-level intellectual expression, mainly between members of the affluent classes, as well as of the foreigners who came to Athens to attend classes in philosophy, and the second is the use of personal wealth to cover the state's total inability to construct public works to improve the life of the populace. Herodes was an orator and a benefactor, who sponsored the building of the Odeum that bears his name and the revetting with marble of the Panathenaic Stadium [fig. 45]. But the weakness of the state is not only apparent in public works. High offices were assumed by members of wealthy families, who were able to cover the costs these entailed, whereas the state and, even more so, ordinary citizens could not. For some time now, the poor had been becoming poorer and the rich richer. This explains why the same persons appear again and again in the inscriptions, either as archons of some authority or as honoured by the *demos*, whose activities were in large part covered by manifestations of honour towards them.

It was in the reign of Marcus Aurelius that the barbarian tribes made their first incursions into the coasts and interior of Greece, and although they were successfully repelled the sanctuary of Eleusis was put to the torch.

In the third century AD the raids from the Balkans proliferated and in AD 267 the Heruls attacked Athens, wreaking havoc, pillaging and reducing to ruins the buildings in the lower city and on the south slope of the Acropolis. Erennius Dexippus managed to repulse them, but the population had suffered serious losses. With the founding of Constantinople as seat of the Eastern Roman Empire and the parallel spread of Christianity, the political and cultural epicentre of the Oecumene shifted gradually to the East, and as the years passed Greece became rather a backwater [fig. 54].

The Greek Dodecatheon was slowly waning and the attempt by emperor Julian the Apostate (AD 360–363) to restore worship of the pagan gods failed. The continuing operation of the philosophical schools gave Athens some breath of life, but the end of the ancient world was nigh [fig. 55]. The death knell came with Justinian's edict (AD 529) banning the teaching of Greek philosophy, with the resultant closure of the schools in Athens.

Henceforth Hellenic civilization was to live on through Byzantium.

56 Athens. The Arch of Hadrian, beside Amalias Avenue, at the height of the sanctuary of Zeus Olympios, was built by the Athenians in honour of the emperor. The arch marks the boundary between the old city and its extension, the new city, which was built by the philhellene emperor. On the west side of the arch, facing the Acropolis, is the inscription: "αἵδ' εἴσ' Ἀθῆναι Θησέως ἡ πρὶν πόλις" (Here lies Athens the old city of Theseus), while on the east: "αἵδ' εἴσ' Ἀνδριανοῦ καὶ οὐχί Θησέως πόλις" (Here lies the city of Hadrian not of Theseus).

56

Athens

PANOS VALAVANIS

Athens appeared on the forestage of History in a very modest manner, which in no way presaged that the small settlements of arable farmers and stock-raisers existing upon and around the rock of the Acropolis by the end of the second millennium BC, would evolve, within a few hundred years, into one of the capital cities of the ancient world.

It is perhaps to these numerous settlements that the plural form of the place name *Athenai* / Athens (see also *Mykenai* / Mycenae, *Thebai* / Thebes, etc.) is due. This toponym must have already existed in prehistoric times, since it originates from a prehellenic linguistic substrate. According to later mythical tradition, the city was named after the goddess Athena, surely an old Minoan and subsequently Mycenaean deity, protectress of the palace, who in the Linear B tablets is referred to as *A-ta-na po-ti-ni-ja*, that is Athena Potnia (revered). Despite the similarity in the names of the goddess and the city, no secure hypotheses can be posited concerning their provenance and correlation. It seems very probable that Athens was initially the name of the Acropolis.

The natural environment of the city had hardly changed since prehistoric times. At the centre of the Athens basin loomed the rock of the Acropolis [fig. 58], at the edges of which the Mycenaean Cyclopean wall was preserved in relatively good condition. In speaking of the ancient city (*asty*), we should not forget the rural territory (*chora*) that surrounded it, Attica, which was full of smaller and larger mixed-farming settlements, some coastal with involvement also in fishing and trade, as well as many smaller settlement units, which were linked to one another and with the capital by a dense network of roads, as well as by ties of political, economic and cultural dependence.

The dissolution of the Mycenaean civilization throughout the Greek Mainland affected Athens too. Information on the Submycenaean period (1100–1050 BC) is gained mainly from the excavation of a few graves in the Agora and of one organized cemetery of about one hundred and fifty graves in the Kerameikos, on the right bank of the River Eridanos [fig. 58]. The number and the form of the graves, as well as the kind of grave goods, point to

57

57 Athens, Kerameikos. Attic amphora of the Protogeometric period (*ca* 950 BC). Found in the Kerameikos cemetery, the vase contained the ashes of the deceased, bearing witness to the change in mortuary customs from inhumation to cremation in Athens, in this period. At the same time, the new tectonic structure of the vase, the harmony between shape and decoration, as well as the geometric character of the decorative motifs (concentric circles and semicircles), exemplify the new concept that appeared in Greek art at the beginning of the 1st millennium BC. Athens, Kerameikos Museum.

an increase in the population, which was, however, much poorer than in Mycenaean times. The settlement that the cemetery served cannot have been far away and was probably located on the gentle slopes of the Acropolis.

Information on the succeeding period, the Protogeometric (1050–900 BC), is drawn again from the Kerameikos, where some fifty graves have been excavated a short distance to the west of the previous cemetery, on the left bank of the Eridanos. However, a radical difference in the burial habits is observed: the dead are no longer inhumed but cremated and their ashes are put in a vase that is placed together with the grave goods inside a burial pit. This "sudden" change in mortuary practices, which are one of the most conservative procedures in cultural history, is difficult to understand. It denotes a change in the religious consciousness of the inhabitants, a phenomenon which earlier research had associated with the change in the composition of the population of Athens, after the so-called Descent of the Dorians. However, the Athenian tradition relating to King Kodros, as well as the indications, in certain artistic manifestations, of a smooth transition from the Submycenaean to the Protogeometric period, weaken the hypothesis of a violent historical watershed.

Nonetheless, in the shape and the decorative motifs of the vases of the new era [fig. 57], the new disciplined tectonic concept is apparent, which points to some cultural change and exemplifies the new dynamism of society. It seems that at that time the new population substrate of Attica, an outcome perhaps of the mixing of the old Mycenaeans with the incomers whose influx was probably peaceful, had begun to be constituted and to develop. These Athenians were to be the agent of the major transformations and the significant achievements of Archaic and Classical times.

The period 900–700 BC has been called Geometric, precisely because of the new geometric concept which was expressed for the first time in Athenian pottery and vase-painting. Its most impressive works are the large vases of the so-called "Dipylon Group", mainly amphorae and kraters, which crowned earth mounds or tumuli that were raised over cremation burials and over inhumations, as this latter practice was gradually resumed. The pioneering role of Athenian pottery in this period, with the introduction of narrative representations [fig. 59], is symptomatic of a wider innovative spirit and bespeaks the city's leading presence in the context of the more general recovery throughout Greece.

Building remains of the Geometric period are scant and point to the existence of a settlement and burials upon the Acropolis, as well as to the north and east of the rock. At the same time, statistical analyses of the graves by period, as well as the continuously increasing number of wells, which are

58 Athens. Aerial photograph of the historical centre of Athens, from the northwest, showing the most important areas of development of the ancient city. In the foreground, the Kerameikos with the fortification wall and the most important gateways (Dipylon and Hiera Pyle), as well as the splendid cemetery. The large rectangular building behind the wall is the Pompeion. In the middle distance, above the Theseion urban railway station, are the temple of Hephaistos and the archaeological site of the Agora. The Panathenaic Way, which runs through the Agora, leads to the Acropolis, while behind the Stoa of Attalos lies the Roman Agora. Top right, in front of the Acropolis, is the Areopagus hill, while visible top left are the columns of the temple of Zeus Olympios.

59

59 Athens. Monumental krater, h. 1.23 m, of the Geometric period (*ca* 740 BC). It belongs, along with several similar vases, to the so-called "Dipylon Group" of large funerary vases that were set up on graves of aristocrats and received libations (choai) in their honour. Developed in successive zones on the body of the vase are the first pictorial scenes in Greek art, with schematic silhouette figures. The usual representations are the prothesis (lying in state) and the ekphora (carrying to the grave) of the dead, accompanied by lamenting women in single file and chariots with armed warriors. Athens, National Archaeological Museum.

assumed to have been located in neighbourhoods or house courtyards, denote a steady rise in population. These data are drawn mainly from the area of the later Agora, which seems to have been used without break as a locus of workshops and burial from 1000 to 600 BC. Another important cemetery of the period has been excavated in the area to the south of the Acropolis, in the neighbourhood of Koukaki, parallel to the present Makrygianni, Falirou and Erechtheiou streets, as well as in Kotzia Square. It seems that already from the early periods, cemeteries had been organized at a distance from the houses and along the main road arteries. The wealth and diversity of the grave goods accompanying the burials attest to economic recovery and increasing contacts with the eastern Mediterranean, as well as to clear social stratification.

The most important achievements at the end of the Geometric period were the constitution of Attica as a single city-state, under the control of Athens, and the instituting of worship of the patron deity, with the aim of reinforcing the political unification of the inhabitants. The direct reference by Homer (*Iliad* II 549, *Odyssey* x 81) to the existence, even in his day, of a temple on the Acropolis, perhaps on the site of the Mycenaean palace, is explicit testimony. Nonetheless, study of the early tiles from the Sacred Rock indicates the existence of two small temples. Concurrently, the retaining and development of many other cults of local or popular character is ascertained in Athens and in the countryside, even though the religious geography of Attica was not crystallized before the seventh century BC.

Later Athenian tradition attributed the historic event of the constitution of Attica as a city-state, in the eighth century BC, to Theseus, who must have been one of the kings of the Mycenaean period [fig. 22]. This is perhaps a conscious anachronism of the Athenians themselves, who desired to link the most important event in their history with their great hero and leader (*archegetes*).

It seems that in the seventh century BC, the Early Archaic period, circumstances were difficult for Athens. The abandonment of many wells in the area of the Agora and the statistics of cemeteries in Attica have been interpreted as indicative of a population decrease in the first half of the century, a phenomenon that had been attributed to protracted drought, which led to epidemics. These indications of decline are reinforced by the lack of significant building remains from the period, as well as by the absence of Athens from the colonial expansion, which was by now at its peak. Although this view has been doubted on good grounds, there is no doubt that the seventh century BC was a time of hardships, with conflicts between aristocratic clans and a climate of political and social upheaval. Even so, the introduction of the phalanx of hoplites, the legislation of Drakon and the creation of the first public spaces gave new impetus to political and social development.

The organization of Attic society in powerful aristocratic clans is also reflected in the Kerameikos cemetery, where the arrangement of graves in large tumuli, in which members of the clans were buried, accompanied by very rich grave goods, is observed during the seventh and sixth centuries BC. Modern research interprets this as a "reactionary" move by the aristocrats and their return to earlier Homeric burial customs.

The seventh century BC is the sole period in which Attica imported more vases, primarily Corinthian, than it exported, although the experiments in so-called Protoattic vase-painting are bold, with mythological subjects appearing for the first time and dominating the entire surface of the vases [fig. 60].

By the dawn of the sixth century BC, Athens was in dire political and social straits, which led the warring factions to the person of Solon. His legislation (594 BC) is a major step in the development of the regime and contributed to the city quickly regaining its forces and to its enhancement as one of the most important city-states in Archaic Greece.

From this time survive the earliest textual testimonies on the function of the body politic, which is also confirmed by the first archaeological evidence for the founding of the Agora, on the smooth slope adjacent to the hill of Agoraios Kolonos, and its formation as the civic centre. The area was not empty ground and, in addition to a few graves, it seems to have been occupied by pottery workshops, as demonstrated by the most recent study of the pottery from deposits and wells hereabouts. Consequently, the Athenian State must have proceeded to gradual expropriations of private spaces for the successive construction of public buildings. The first public buildings were found under the foundations of the Classical Bouleuterion (Council House) and are thought to have housed the *Boule* (Council) of Four Hundred, instituted by Solon.

Until then, the seat of authority and of the various institutions of the Athenian State was located on the Acropolis and, perhaps from the seventh century BC, in some public buildings that had been erected on its northeast slope. This area of Athens, which later Athenians named "Agora of Theseus" to distinguish it from the Agora of Classical times or "of Solon", included many public edifices, such as the Boukoleion, the Thesmotheteion and the Prytaneion, in which the Legal Code of Solon had been set up for public view. There were sanctuaries here too, such as the Thesmophoreion, the Anakeion (sanctuary of the Dioskouroi) and the Theseion, which was founded by Kimon after 476/5 BC. As yet, no clear architectural remains have been ascribed to these buildings, due to the limited excavation research in the Plaka neighbourhood. In general, the area of the early Agora is located

60

60 Protoattic amphora, h. 1.42 m, found in the ancient cemetery of Eleusis, where it had been used for the burial of a child. During the 7th century BC, Athenian vase-painters took the bold step of representing for the first time mythological subjects in large compositions. Depicted on the neck of the vase is the Blinding of Polyphemos by Odysseus and his companions, while on the body is Perseus beheading Medusa. Athens, National Archaeological Museum.

61

between present Adrianou and Tripodon streets, although a recent theory proposes that the ruins in Agia Aikaterini Square, in Lysikratous Street, should be identified as of the Prytaneion.

During the early sixth century BC (590–580 BC), it seems that the first monumental temple, the first *Hekatompedon*, was founded on the Acropolis, in the place of what would later be known as the Parthenon, while in the *Asty*, in the area of the Olympieion, there was perhaps a Doric temple, the foundations of which (31x60 m) have been found under the later temple. Concurrently, the appearance of monumental sculpture in this period led to the creation of the first statues of kouroi and korai, which were erected throughout the century, either as votive offerings in the major sanctuaries (Acropolis, Sounion), or as funerary sculptures [figs 61, 64] in the cemeteries of city-dwellers (Kerameikos) or of landowners (Mesogaia). Also, the development of black-figure vase-painting and the production of excellent-quality pottery [fig. 62] brought the increase in exports and the gradual domination of Attica in the international markets, mainly to the detriment of its competitor Corinth, which gave a big boost to the Athenian economy.

From 565–510 BC, Athens was ruled by Peisistratos and his sons. This was a period of great economic growth and prosperity, due to the tyrants' large-scale public building projects, the revitalizing of many cults, the support of manufacturing and the export of its products. The existence of strong central authority and accumulated wealth are the two factors that favoured the development of monumental art, and these decades were one of the most productive phases of artistic creation in Attica.

During the tyranny the Acropolis evolved into a flourishing sanctuary, richly adorned with temples and statues, remains of which were found built into the Classical fortification wall as *spolia*, or buried in pits. This was considered to be due either to the Persian destruction, or to a deliberate destruction of them by the Athenians themselves, immediately after the abolition of the tyranny.

These remains have generated a contentious debate on the form of the Archaic Acropolis: in the view of one group of scholars, there were two large poros peripteral temples on the sacred rock in the sixth century BC (the *Archaic Parthenon* and the temple referred to in the sources as the "Old Temple" [*Archaios Neos*]), in which two different hypostases of Athena were worshipped and which were precursors of the Classical Parthenon and the Erechtheion respectively. The other group argues, though less persuasively, that just one temple existed, the foundations of which still survive to the south of the Erechtheion. The rest of the architectural and sculptural members are thought to belong to a group of five-six smaller edifices (*oikoi*), perhaps intended for the cult of Athenian heroes, such as Kekrops and

Erechtheus. Most of the pedimental sculptures are dated *circa* the mid-sixth century BC and render subjects from the Labours of Herakles, which fact is interpreted as one of the first uses of the hero for political propaganda by the tyrants. After 525 BC the large temple was reconstructed as peripteral, with 6x12 columns, and for the first time acquired marble pediments, represented on one of which was the Gigantomachy [fig. 101]. Lately, the date of this temple, which is dubbed "of the Peisistratids", has been lowered and its attribution to the young Athenian democracy has been proposed.

Shortly before the middle years of the sixth century BC, the Archaic Propylaia of the Acropolis were built and worship of Athena Nike was established, with the construction of a small temple and an altar upon the tower of the Mycenaean Cyclopean wall [fig. 88]. This programme is associated with the reorganization of the Panathenaic festival, probably by Peisistratos, an intervention of seminal importance at a time when the Athenians were becoming aware of the significant political role of the principal festivals and athletics games. In the same period, the area of the Acropolis was full of *ex-votos*, mainly korai statues, which were dedicated most probably by prominent aristocratic clans, whose daughters served the cult of Athena [figs 65, 97, 98].

Peisistratos and his sons are also associated with the transfer of the cult of Artemis Brauronia to upon the Sacred Rock, and of Dionysos to the south slope of the Acropolis, as well as the instituting of the Great Dionysia festival. They are accredited too with the initiative of constructing a colossal Doric dipteral temple of Zeus Olympios, the largest temple in metropolitan Greece. This had reached the height of about 8 m when the tyranny was toppled and work stopped. In 479 BC, part of its material (some 30 poros column drums) was used to construct a gateway in the Themistoclean forti- fication wall.

The tyrants also showed interest in the Agora, and it has been suggested recently that they were responsible for its first spatial layout, not as a locus of political activities, but of athletics and artistic ones, as well as a parade ground for the Athenian infantry and cavalry. Dated to their rule is the founding of the first Eleusinion and the construction of the so-called Building F, which has the plan of a large house and may have been the residence of the tyrants' family, who had by now come down from the Acropolis. Thus, the Sacred Rock was transformed from the seat of rulers to the exclusively religious centre of the city. In 522/1 BC, as Thucydides (6.55) records, the altar of the Twelve Gods was set up, while the monumental fountain "of the nine spouts", the Ennea-

61 Athens. Attic grave stele (510–500 BC) with relief representation of the hoplite Aristion. A work by the sculptor Aristokles, as is inscribed on the lower part of the stele. Archaic art, with its restrained majesty, attained its most splendid expression in Athens in the 6th century BC. The appearance of the names of artists, who proudly signed their creations, bespeaks the importance attached to the personality of the individual, a fundamental value in ancient Greek society. Athens, National Archaeological Museum.

62, 63 Athens. Two characteristic vases of the pottery production of Athens in the Late Archaic period, which was not only one of the highest forms of artistic expression, but also a significant factor in the city's economy. Left, black-figure amphora of 530 BC, work of Exekias, with representation of the Dioskouroi, Kastor and Polydeukes (Pollux), being received by their parents, Leda and Tyndareus. Vatican, Museo Gregoriano Etrusco. Right, red-figure amphora of 490 BC, work of the so-called Berlin Painter, with a superb composition of Hermes, a hind and a Satyr. Berlin, Antikenmuseum, Staatliche Museen Preußischer Kulturbesitz.

62

63

64 Athens, Kerameikos. The destruction of the city by the Persians in 480 BC, shortly before the naval battle of Salamis, has been documented by excavations in many places, particularly in the Kerameikos cemetery. In spring 2002, just outside the Hiera Pyle (Sacred Gate), an unexpected new find was uncovered, enriching the collection of Archaic funerary sculptures in the Kerameikos Museum. One kouros, two sphinxes and one lion adorned a tomb monument of the early 6th century BC, prior to its obliteration by the enemies some 100 years after it had been founded. After the devastation, the Athenians used the sculptures to reinforce the infrastructure of the Hiera Pyle, which at this particular point was susceptible to flooding by the waters of the River Eridanos.

krounos, was constructed at about this time, as part of a wider plan to supply the city with water. Sections of the pipes that brought water from a source on Mount Hymettos were uncovered in recent excavations. The tyrants should be credited too with founding the three public gymnasia in Athens, the Akademia (Academy), the Lykeion (Lyceum) and the Kynosarges.

Around 530–520 BC, a new artistic invention of the Athenians came to boost not only art but also the economy. This was the creation of the red-figure style in vase-painting, which gave great impetus to the development of pottery, promoting the Athenian workshops as paramount exporting centres which dominated the markets, crushing their commercial competitors [fig. 63].

64

The period from the founding of the Athenian democracy in 508/7 BC, on the initiative of Kleisthenes, to the destruction of the city by the Persians in 480 BC, is distinguished by the first implementation of the new regime. The new institutions led correspondingly to the development of the Agora as focus of public life and political activity of the state. In the same period, an open-air semicircular area was arranged on the Pnyx, where, after the democratic reforms, all Athenian citizens assembled to hear the proposals and to vote on decisions that regulated their city's political affairs.

In the Agora, construction of several new buildings commenced, such as the Bouleuterion to house the new *Boule* of the Five Hundred, and the Royal (Basileios) Stoa, as seat of the *archon basileus*, one of the ten annually elected archons of the new body politic. On the west side, at the foot of Agoraios Kolonos hill, small sanctuaries were built in honour of Zeus, Apollo, the Mother of the Gods, while on the north side a marble altar was erected to Aphrodite Ourania. Architectural remains are so scant that the existence of some of these sanctuaries has been doubted, while the identification of the altar is also problematical. Shortly after 500 BC, the first theatral building in history still simple was created above the sanctuary of Dionysos.

The most important event in monumental architecture of this period, immediately after the battle of Marathon (490 BC), was the beginning of the construction, on the Acropolis, of a large marble temple in honour of Athena, who had saved the city from the barbarian attack. It was located on the site of the subsequent Parthenon, for which reason it is known to scholarship as the *Vorparthenon*, and was the first temple constructed entirely of marble from Mount Pentele, where the quarries had been recently established. But works were cut short at the level of the third drum of the columns, perhaps as soon as the Athenians learnt of the Persians' preparations for a second campaign, under Xerxes. The unfinished edifice was burnt when the Persians put the Acropolis to the torch, together with all the architectural works, sculptures and other *ex-votos* on the Sacred Rock. After their victories at Salamis (480 BC) and Plataiai (479 BC), and the fending off of the Persian threat, one of the Athenians' first concerns was to clear the destroyed sanctuaries [fig. 65]. Those remnants that were in good condition were buried in pits, from which they were recovered in the excavations of 1883–1886, and the unfinished members of the *Vorparthenon* were incorporated into the north fortification wall of the Acropolis, where they can be seen to this day [fig. 90].

The picture of the Persian destruction of the city is documented archaeologically in the Agora too, by levels with remains of public and private buildings, while in the Kerameikos, the discovery of many Archaic grave statues and stelai built into the Themistoclean wall shows that the invaders did not even respect the tombs.

After the resounding victories over the Persians, Athens emerged as hegemonic city, as well as cultural and artistic centre of the Hellenic world. The coexistence of perspicacious leaders, gifted artists, a conscientious citizen body, due to the development of democracy and abundant economic means, led to the creation of great works and splendid artistic achievements in the fifth century BC. The fact that this period is dubbed "Classical" denotes the elevation of the city and its creations to a model, the yardstick by which all preceding and succeeding civilizations would henceforth be evaluated. The most characteristic expression of this period are the architectural works in the major building project of the Athenian State, which produced no less than twelve temples and other monumental edifices in Attica as a whole.

However, prior to the implementation of this project, the city's security had precedence. So, on the initiative of Themistocles, the years immediately after the repulsion of the Persian foe were devoted to constructing the new fortified enceinte that rose like a protective ring, some 6.5 kilometres in length, around the city, enclosing an area no larger than 170–200 hectares [fig. 66]. It circumvallated all the residential areas, most of the sanctuaries and, of course, the Agora. There were thirteen main gates, opened on pre-existing roads that led to the *demoi* outside the *Asty* and to the countryside. As part of the same undertaking, the Piraeus was fortified [figs 175, 176] and was henceforth the main port of Athens. The programme of fortification works in Athens was completed by the leaders who succeeded Themistocles, namely Kimon and Pericles, who put up the Long Walls as well as the so-called Phaleron Wall. Concurrently, the Classical wall of the Acropolis was

65 Athens. Kore no. 675 (*ca* 510 BC) is one of the 200 or so korai statues that had been dedicated on the Acropolis in the course of the 6th century BC. These were probably ex-votos of aristocratic clans of the city, offered on the occasion of their daughters' service in the sanctuary of Athena. They were destroyed when the Persians put to the torch the Sacred Rock, and were subsequently placed by the Athenians in a pit near the Erechtheion, where they were found during the large-scale excavations in 1883–1886. The pigments preserved on the statue hint at the splendid polychromy of ancient sculpture. Athens, Acropolis Museum.

65

66 Athens. Model of the city of Athens intra muros, the so-called Asty. The Themistoclean wall, approximately 6.5 km long, enclosed the entire settled area, the most important sanctuaries and public spaces. At intervals, and on the pre-existing road axes, 13 gateways were opened, which led to the demoi outside the Asty, in the countryside of Attica, and to the rest of Greece. The initial enceinte reached as far as the Olympieion and was extended eastwards in Roman times, in order to include the later expansion of the city. Athens, Acropolis Study Centre.

built, not so much as a rampart but as a sanctuary enclosure (*peribolos*). It projected some way beyond the brink of the rock, thus functioning also as a retaining wall, containing the earth with which the surface of the rock had been widened appreciably, so as to accommodate the large monuments of the new building project [figs 67, 73, 90].

Predictably, the epicentre of the architectural activity of the Athenian State, which commenced in the mid-fifth century BC, was the Acropolis, which had lain destroyed for thirty years. The project was planned by Pericles himself and his coterie of politicians and artists, but in accordance with the democratic processes it had to be vetted and approved by the relevant bodies of the Athenian State, that is the *boule* and the *ekklesia* of the *demos*, as was the case with all public works. The aim of this programme was to construct three temples in honour of the three hypostases of the goddess Athena (Polias, Parthenos, Nike), as well as a monumental gateway (Propylaia). It lasted, with interruptions, for the entire second half of the fifth century BC.

66

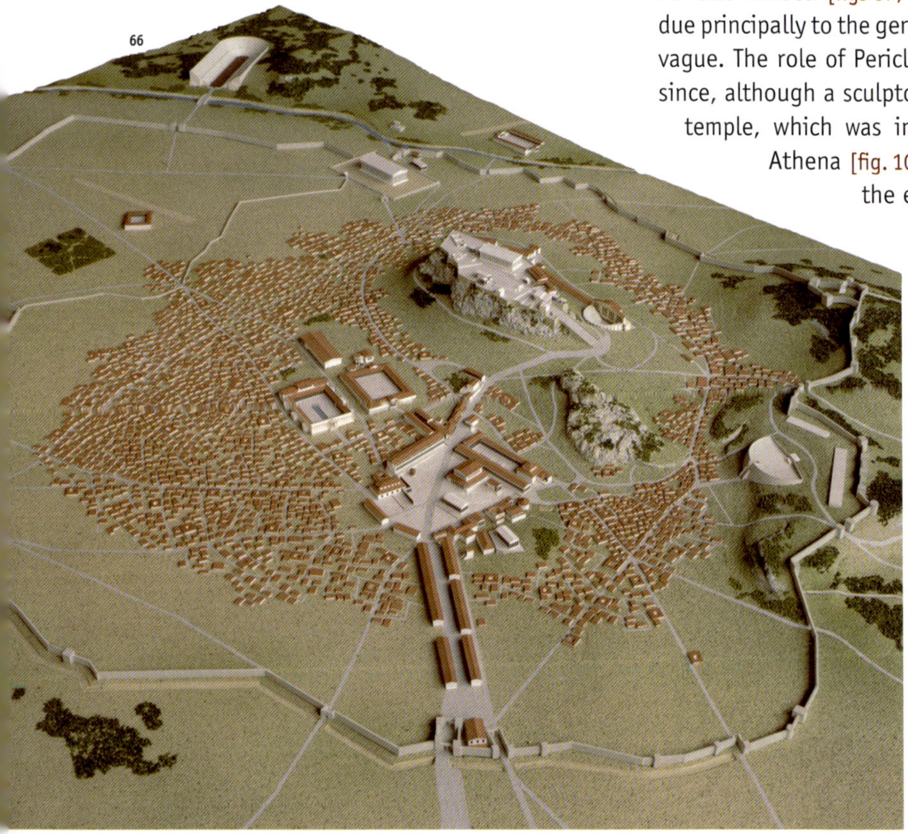

The first works, the Parthenon (447–432 BC) and the Propylaia (437–432 BC), were erected within a relatively short time and were inaugurated by Pericles himself [figs 67, 73, 90, 118, 121]. The design of the Parthenon was due principally to the genius of Iktinos, while the input of Kallikrates remains vague. The role of Pericles' friend Pheidias must have been important too, since, although a sculptor, he appears to have influenced the plans for the temple, which was intended to house his chryselephantine statue of Athena [fig. 108]. With its harmonious architectural proportions, the exquisite quality of its craftsmanship and its sculptural decoration, the Parthenon is not only a building unsurpassed in conception and execution, but also the symbol of the Athenian democracy. According to the most recent research, incorporated in its north pteron was a pre-existing Archaic *naiskos*, while in the east wall of the cella were windows, the first in an ancient temple for the better illumination of the interior and the better visibility of the ivory-and-gold statue.

Mnesikles' design for the Propylaia [figs 67, 73, 90, 121] seems to have been implemented in part in the south wing, while in the north the so-called *Pinakotheke* was created, probably as a banquet hall for the sucrifice of the Panathenaia recreation of official visitors to the Acropolis. The building was never completed, perhaps because of the outbreak of the Peloponnesian War.

The Erechtheion (421–415 BC and 410–406 BC) and the temple of Athena Nike (426–421 BC) were constructed with interruptions, during lulls in the Peloponnesian War. The first has a peculiar appearance with three porches, four different fronts and a divided interior, because in it were accommodated the cults of different deities, heroes and kings of Athenian mythical tradition [figs 69, 117]. It was shifted to the north of the earlier destroyed temple that it succeeded, perhaps in order to leave free the central part of the rock, thus creating the essential space where thousands of Athenians congregated during the great *hecatomb* (sacrifice of 100 oxen) that concluded the Panathenaic festival. At the same time, the tower in the Mycenaean fortification wall, upon which the temple of Athena Nike stands, was revetted with isodomic masonry, leaving an aperture at the base, through which the Cyclopean wall could be seen, as witness to the city's glorious past [fig. 88]. According to a very recent theory, it is possible that on the tower, as a kind of trophy, were hung the shields of Spartan captives taken in the battle of Sphakteria (426 BC), which the Athenians displayed with great pride.

The sculptural decoration [figs 68–72, 88, 105, 107] of these monuments, on the pediments, metopes and friezes (Parthenon: Birth of Athena, Quarrel between Athena and Poseidon, Amazonomachy, Centauromachy, Gigantomachy, Fall of Troy, the Panathenaic Procession; Erechtheion: myths of old kings and heroes of Athens. Temple of Athena Nike: Battles between Greeks and Trojans or Athenians and Persians) transmitted explicit political messages, aimed on the one hand at proclaiming the autochthony of the Athenians, and on the other of extolling their role in victories over mythical and historical enemies, thus documenting their right to the panhellenic hegemony.

These important conceptions of Pericles and their application by the Athenian democracy not only fulfilled their objective but also achieved something their creators could never have imagined; they surpassed time, surviving through the ages, and have been enhanced as works *non pareil* of climactic moments in the intellectual and artistic expression of the history of civilization.

In this same period, the second Theatre of Dionysos was built on the south slope of the Acropolis, as well as the Odeion of Pericles, a spacious closed auditorium (4,000 sq. m.), surely the first "concert hall" in history [fig.

67

67 Athens. Model of the Acropolis (work of architect M. Korres), with all the architectural works of the grand building programme of the Athenian State in the second half of the 5th century BC. The first buildings constructed were in the Doric order — the Parthenon and the Propylaia —, and were followed by those in the Ionic order — the temple of Athena Nike and the Erechtheion —, all with marble roofs. Humbler are the Π-shaped sanctuary of Artemis Brauronia and the Arrephoreion, next to the north wall. Predominant in the middle is the bronze statue of Athena Promachos, by Pheidias. At the foot of the rock, below the Propylaia, is a small sanctuary of Aphrodite, while half way up the south slope is the Ionic Stoa of the sanctuary of Asklepios.

68, 69 Athens, Acropolis. The Erechtheion, a composite building lacking in uniformity, was created in order to house very ancient relics from the city's prehistoric past, remnants of the primeval cults of the Athenians, as well as sacred signs of divine presence on the Acropolis, such as the olive tree of Athena, the water saurce of Poseidon and the traces of the thunderbolt of Zeus. The porch with the Korai (Karyatids) stands over a prehistoric tomb, which the ancient Athenians believed was that of Kekrops, and partly upon the foundations of the Archaic temple of Athena, which are visible in the foreground. The original statues have been removed from the monument and are exhibited in the Acropolis Museum.

68

73]. In 421/0 BC, on the same slope, the sanctuary of Asklepios [fig. 116] was founded by a citizen, while in the area of the River Ilissos the first Ionic temple in mainland Greece, dedicated to Artemis Agrotera, was built shortly after the mid-fifth century BC (445–435 BC). This displayed similarities to the slightly later temple of Athena Nike on the Acropolis and survived, converted into a church, until 1778, when it was demolished by the Turks [fig. 123], as a result of which only scant remnants of its foundations can now be traced.

During the second quarter of the fifth century BC, on the initiative of Kimon, the Athenian State took measures to rehabilitate the Agora, which had been devastated by the Persians. Old buildings had to be reconstructed and new ones erected, to serve the functions of the goverment. In this context, the Royal Stoa and the old Bouleuterion were rebuilt, while constructed for the first time were the Tholos, as seat of the Prytaneis, the main body of the city's executive authority, and the Poikile or Painted Stoa, which according to another interpretation may be the Stoa of the Herms. In the middle years of the century, the temple of Hephaistos (the so-called Theseion) was built adjacent to the Agora, while the new Bouleuterion, the Stoa of Zeus, the so-called South Stoa I and the Mint date from the last quarter of the century [figs 76, 132].

Two recent archaeological finds shed new light on episodes in Athenian history in this period: the first is the excavation at the corner of Peiraios and Iera Odos streets (the ancient Hiera Hodos or Sacred Way), of a mass grave of about 180 individuals, which has been attributed to victims of the plague epidemic in Athens during the Peloponnesian War, to which Thucydides refers [figs 74, 75]. The second is the discovery of parts of a *polyandrion*, that is a public tomb monument, at 35 Salaminos Street, which has been attributed to Athenians slain in some of the first battles of the decade 430–420 BC.

The end of the Peloponnesian War (404 BC), with the odious terms of peace, as well as the brief tyranny of the Thirty, which lasted a few months, left Athens badly wounded. Even so, around 400 BC a large multi-purpose public building, the Pompeion [fig. 58], was constructed in the Kerameikos, between the Dipylon and the Sacred Gate (Hiera Pyle). This functioned at once as a gymnasium and as a repository for organizing and safekeeping the sacred paraphernalia of the Panathenaic procession. It also had rooms for official banquets for the city's guests, who dined on the meat of the sacrificed animals, after the end of the great festival.

A few years later, in 393–390 BC, the Athenians, under their leader Konon, exploited Persian monies and rebuilt the long walls and the walls of the Piraeus [fig. 174], which the Spartans had destroyed, thus simultaneously regaining their injured pride. Concurrently, they built on the Acropolis the Chalkotheke, an edifice to house the metal votive offerings of the sanctuary.

70–72 Athens. The sculpted decoration of the Classical buildings on the Acropolis, which was developed on the pediments, the metopes, the friezes and the akroteria of the temples, drew on the mythological repertoire, which was used to transmit political messages of the Athenian State. Sole exception is the Parthenon frieze, represented on which is an actual event, the splendid procession of the Panathenaia. However, this too is a hymn to the superiority of the Athenian State and its citizens, since through its structure and division it reflects on one long side the organization of the city in the period before Kleisthenes' reforms, and on the other the democratic organization of the city-state in the time of Pericles, so aiming at a harmonious conjugation of the past with the present.

70 Block from the north Parthenon frieze, with the hydriaphoroi (pitcher-bearers) carrying on their shoulders offerings for the goddess. Athens, Acropolis Museum.

71 Block from the north Parthenon frieze, with two horsemen cantering to the left. Highly impressive is the rythmical superimposition of men and animals, especially their legs. London, British Museum.

72 Block from the south Parthenon frieze, with three youths driving an unsettled oxen to be sacrificed, which with its head raised lets out a moo. London, British Museum.

70

According to the latest research, it seems that in the decade 370–360 BC renovation of the sanctuary of Dionysos commenced [figs 73, 114] and construction of the new and larger theatre, which is known as the Theatre of Lykourgos, because it was completed in 340–330 BC, when he was archon. The same notable leader is also accredited with the building of the Panathenaic Stadium [figs 45, 66]. Thus, events celebrated in connection with the city's two most important festivals, the Great Dionysia and the Panathenaia, acquired monumental venues. In the same period, the Pnyx was remodelled and the sanctuary of Asklepios was improved for the first time, with a temple and a two-storey stoa [figs 73, 116]. In his effort to stress the importance of the old institutions of the Athenian State, Lykourgos built in the Agora the temple of Apollo Patroos and the temple of Zeus Phratrios and Athena Phratria, and re-founded for a second time a purely political monument, that of the ten eponymous heroes of the Athenian tribes, which was an artistic expression of the tribal constitution of the Athenian democracy. Lykourgos also built the palaestra in the Lykeion (Lyceum) Gymnasium, which was excavated of late in Rigillis Street, while in all probability he attempted to continue construction of the temple of Zeus Olympios, in marble. The archonship of Lykourgos was the last period of major public works that were decided upon and funded by the Athenian State.

However, the fourth century BC was also a time of works that conspicuously displayed private wealth, a phenomenon that signalled the shaking of the

71

72

73 Athens. Aerial view of the Acropolis and its environs, from the south. The initially small flat surface of the rock was widened considerably by the construction of the north (Themistoclean) and the south (Kimonean) fortification wall, which functioned also as a retaining wall on which the new large buildings of the Classical period stood. Upon the rock there is still the worksite serving the major restoration project. Dominating the edges of the south slope are the Theatre of Dionysos, right, and the Odeum of Herodes Atticus, left, which are "linked" by the retaining wall of the Stoa of Eumenes. Visible above the stoa and the theatre is the Peripatos, the walkway that runs round the foot of the rock. High above the Theatre of Dionysos are the remains of the choregic monuments of Thrasyllos and of his son Thrasykles (on the rock), as well as two columns from other choregic monuments, while a little way to the left are the stoas of the Asklepieion. Left of the Acropolis is the hill of the Areopagus and above is the archaeological site of the Agora, with a part of the Stoa of Attalos. The picture of today's neighbourhood of Plaka, with the single-storey, tiled-roof houses, is probably little different from that of the residential tissue of the ancient city.

74

74, 75 Athens. Vases from the mass grave of about 180 dead, in a pit at the edge of the Kerameikos cemetery, which has been attributed to victims of the plague that struck Athens during the Peloponnesian War, referred to by Thucydides. The grave goods were meagre, while the skeletons were found in total disorder, a state documenting the ancient historian's account. Examination of the DNA of the dead showed that in all probability the illness described as a plague was typhoid fever. Athens, Kerameikos Museum.

foundations of the city-state. Characteristic examples of this trend are the choregic monuments of Lysikrates in the present neighbourhood of Plaka, and of Thrasyllos on the lower slopes of the Acropolis, above the Theatre of Dionysos [fig. 73]. Another expression of the same trend is the sumptuous grave reliefs from the cemeteries of Attica, particularly the Kerameikos [fig. 77]. This splendid artistic output came to an abrupt end between 317 and 307 BC, when Demetrios Phalereus issued a decree limiting the luxury of mortuary monuments [fig. 48].

In the ensuing years, Athens ceased to be an autonomous political entity and was included in the network of relations and conflicts between other mightier powers. Initially of the Diadochoi, the successors to Alexander the Great, that is, the rulers of the Hellenistic kingdoms, in the clashes between them, and subsequently in their clashes with the ascendant power of Rome.

In the framework of these conflicts, towards the end of the fourth century BC and probably in the interval 307–304 BC, the city's fortification wall was restored and reinforced. In front of the existing enceinte, which was strengthened, a low outwork was constructed and a deep moat was dug, as part of the efforts to combat the new siege methods, with the use of catapults and other machines, which were widespread from the fourth century BC. Demetrios Poliorketes, who stayed in Athens and confronted the forces of Kassander of Macedonia, should be accredited with these measures. At the same time, the Diateichisma was constructed, a long cross-wall that passed over the crest of the hills of the Mouseion (Philopappos), the Pnyx and the Nymphs (Observatory), restricting the area on the south side of the city from the long course of the Themistoclean enceinte, which originally came down as far as the modern neighbourhoods of Koukaki and Petralona.

The third century BC was a time of internal political strife, which led to the city's marked decline. Many houses were abandoned, while hardly any public works were undertaken. The most important of these are the square peristyle of side 35 m, on the east side of the Agora, perhaps the seat of law courts, and a large rectangular hypostyle hall next to the temple of Hephaistos, which has been interpreted as an arsenal. It was in this period too that two more gymnasia were founded in the city, one with a donation from Ptolemy III, after 229 BC, and another, the Diogeneion, which was named after the then commander of the Macedonian garrison stationed in Athens. According to a recent theory, the two names refer to one and the same gymnasium complex, which it locates in Plaka, parallel to present Kyrrhestou Street.

75

In the second century BC, there was a significant recovery and a building boom in the city. This was due to its increased importance as a cultural and educational centre for the entire Mediterranean, since Athens was home to the most famous philosophical schools, which had been founded in the fourth century BC by Plato, Aristotle, Zenon and others. Whoever aspired to being considered cultivated and intellectual in this period studied in Athens. Among the students were the scions of royal houses of the Hellenistic East, who, when they became kings, were wont to finance major public works in Athens, on the one hand in recognition of its status as intellectual hearth of the then-known world, and on the other for reasons of political propaganda generated by Rome's expansionism to the East. It is to these potentates that the upsurge in building activity was due during the second century BC, which led to a total remodelling of the city's public places.

The Eastern rulers concentrated on the Agora, where the construction of the Stoa of Attalos on the east side [figs 58, 78, 132], a quadrilateral building complex on the south (Middle Stoa, South Stoa II, East Building) and the new Metroon on the west, created a new layout, giving the square a "mod-

76 Athens. The site of the ancient Agora, hub of the Athenians' political, economic and social activity, photographed from the Acropolis. Top left is the temple of Hephaistos, in commanding position atop Agoraios Kolonos hill. In front of it, on the west side of the Agora, are the foundations of administrative buildings of the city, most of them works of the Classical period. Running obliquely across the square are rows of column drums from the Middle Stoa, which together with the Stoa of Attalos (visible at the bottom right edge) were benefactions of Hellenistic rulers in the 2nd century BC. The white columns in the middle and on the right are three of the giants of the façade of the second phase of the Odeum of Agrippa (2nd c. AD). The church of the Holy Apostles was a parish church of the neighbourhood that covered the archaeological site from the 10th century AD until 1931, when expropriations and systematic excavations commenced.

76

77 Athens. The funerary relief from the tomb of the family of Dexileos, in the Kerameikos, is one of the loveliest works of the early 4th century BC. Represented is a youth on horseback, who is about to thrust his spear into a foe. The inscription on the pedestal records that Dexileos was slain at the age of 20 years, in 394 BC, in a battle fought near Corinth. He was not buried in this tomb but together with other fellow fighters, in a communal grave in the Demosion Sema, in accordance with the ancestral laws of the Athenian State for those who fell in war. Athens, Kerameikos Museum.

ern" image of regular planning and magnificence [fig. 76]. The same was true of the south slope of the Acropolis, which the exceptionally long Stoa of Eumenes II endowed with a monumental aspect, while concurrently serving the needs of the Theatre of Dionysos, which in this period also functioned as seat of the *ekklesia* of the *demos*, instead of the Pnyx [fig. 73]. Consistent with this spirit was the construction, probably by the Ptolemies, of the Horologion of Andronikos Kyrrhestos (Tower of the Winds), which has of late been dated to after the mid-second century BC [fig. 81], as well as the unsuccessful attempt by Antiochos IV of Syria to complete the large temple of Zeus Olympios.

The subjugation of the whole of southern Greece to the Romans, after the battle of Corinth in 146 BC, had little impact on the city. A more important pivotal date in the monumental topography of Athens is 86 BC, when it suffered the catastrophic consequences of the siege by the Roman general Sulla, in reprisal for it having sided with the rival of Rome, King Mithridates of Pontos. Victims of the Romans' rage were the city walls, several buildings in the Agora, the Pompeion in the Kerameikos, as well as the Odeion of Pericles, which was however soon rebuilt with a donation from the King of Cappadocia, Ariobarzanes II. Sulla also felled the trees in the sacred groves of the Lyceum and the Academy, in order to build siege machines, while he took back with him to Rome not only numerous works of art but also the entire library of Aristotle.

From the time of Julius Caesar, and more so of Octavian Augustus, the Romans showed significant interest in Athens, which is also recorded in the contemporary writings of Cicero, Ovid and Horace. This interest was expressed concretely in the creation of a new Roman Agora, to the east of the Classical one, to which all commercial activity was transferred and which became a new hub of social life [figs 81, 132]. In the now free centre of the Classical Agora, an important educational and cultural venue was built, the Odeum of Agrippa [fig. 76].

Upon the Acropolis, a small circular monopteral edifice was erected, usually referred to as the temple of Roma and Augustus, which is alternatively interpreted as an altar for worship of the emperor [figs 53, 120]. The imposition of imperial cult in all cities in Roman territory led to considerable activity in the Agora too, in the latter years of the first century BC. In order to quickly cover the new cultic needs, the Athenians preferred to transfer to the city

77

old temples from the Attic countryside, which seem to have been neglected, instead of building new ones. A fifth-century BC temple of Ares was moved piece by piece to the Agora [fig. 132]. This was thought to have been located originally in Acharnai, but it has recently been proposed that it should be identified with the temple of Athena Pallenis, the infrastructure of which has been found at Pallene. Furthermore, the altar of Zeus Agoraios was transferred from the Pnyx, parts of an unfinished building were moved from Thorikos, and parts of the temple of Athena were brought from Sounion and incorporated in new temples, which were placed amidst the existing buildings. Two temple-shaped chambers behind the Stoa of Zeus Eleutherios also served the needs of worship.

By AD 67, when Nero visited Athens, the orchestra of the Theatre of Dionysos had been remodelled and a new multi-storey *scaenae frons* had been installed [fig. 114]. Later, in the early second century AD, the Library of Pantainos was built in the Agora [figs 52, 132], while constructed on the summit of the hill of the Muses was the mausoleum of Philopappos, Prince of Commagene in Syria, who spent his life in Athens and in recognition of his many gifts to the *demos* was granted the right to build his monumental tomb in this conspicuous position, in AD 114–116 [fig. 82].

The second century AD was an important period for the monumental architecture of the city, thanks to the philhellenism of the Roman emperors, particularly Hadrian [fig. 80], and to the generosity of the magnate and benefactor Herodes Atticus [fig. 79].

The completion, in the Corinthian order, of the temple of Zeus Olympios, is attributed to imperial initiative. It was enclosed within a monumental rectangular *peribolos* and inaugurated in the presence of Hadrian in AD 131/2, while the Athenians honoured the emperor with a triumphal arch, known as the Arch of Hadrian, as well as by creating a new tribe, the Hadrianis [figs 56, 90]. Hadrian financed the construction of a temple dedicated to Zeus Panhellenios, to the south of the Olympieion, of the Pantheon, a sanctuary for all the gods, perhaps in present Adrianou Street, as well as the Library that bears his name, a huge building covering 8,000 sq. m., to the north of the Roman Agora [fig. 132], which as the latest excavations have shown was built upon a thriving

78

78 Athens. View of the interior of the restored Stoa of Attalos, two-storeyed and of double width, with twenty-two shops at the rear (2nd c. BC). This was a public building of commercial character, in which the Athenian State leased shops to tradesmen. At the same time, it was an ideal space for Athenians to assemble and to meet and mingle. Reconstruction of the stoa, in 1953–1956, by the American School of Classical Studies at Athens, under the supervision of architect I. Travlos, not only provided the Agora with a museum but also gives visitors the opportunity to experience something of the atmosphere of such a typical monument of ancient Greek architecture.

79

80

79, 80 Athens. The Athenian magnate and philosopher Herodes Atticus (above) and the Roman emperor Hadrian (below) were two personalities whose benefactions shaped the city's image in the 2nd century AD. Athens, National Archaeological Museum.

Late Hellenistic neighbourhood. A major benefaction for the city was the construction of an enormous aqueduct, which brought water from springs on Mount Parnes to the reservoir on Lykabettos Hill (today Dexameni Square in Kolonaki), from where it was channelled to public fountains throughout Athens. The abundant water enabled the construction of numerous public bathhouses (*balnea* or *thermae*), remains of which have been revealed in recent excavations.

All this architectural activity, which gave the city a new image of prosperity, was part of a wider plan by the emperor to elevate Athens as seat of the Panhellenion, an institution in which Greek and Roman values were merged.

It was in this same period that Herodes Atticus endowed the city with two important benefactions, which, renovated, are still in use today. The first was the revetting with Pentelic marble of the Panathenaic Stadium, for the games of the Panathenaia in AD 143 [fig. 45]. The impressive new stadium could accommodate 50,000 spectators and access to it was facilitated by a three-arched bridge spanning the River Ilissos. On either side of the stadium, on the hilltops of Ardettos, a temple of Tyche (Fortuna) was founded, housing a chryselephantine statue, as well as a long podium on which the Panathenaic ship of the festival was placed. The second major work of Herodes was the construction of the Odeum on the south slope of the Acropolis, which took place in the decade AD 160–170, after the death of his wife Regilla. This was a venue for musical events as well as scholarly lectures and could hold an audience of 6,000 [figs 73, 120]. It was recently proven that the Herodion was originally roofed by a gigantic construction made from wood and terracotta tiles.

The calm, indolent life of the city, in the security guaranteed by the *Pax Romana*, was cut short abruptly and tragically in the following century by the incursion of the Heruls, a Germanic tribe that invaded the lands of the Roman Empire. Despite the strengthening of the fortification by Emperor Valerian, in AD 267, the barbarians attacked the city, pillaging and burning everything. Traces of the destruction can be seen in the Parthenon, on the south slope of the Acropolis and, primarily, in the buildings of the Agora, most of which were literally razed.

This disaster changed the city's character and the consequent dramatic decrease in population is reflected in the area that those Athenians who survived fortified a few years later. It included only the north slope of the Acropolis, as far as the Library of Hadrian, as well as the upper parts of the east and south slopes. The west side of this Late Roman fortification wall, which reached up to the Stoa of Attalos, was built entirely of *spolia* from the ruinous buildings of the Agora, which for the first time in its history remained *extra muros*. The Acropolis acquired a new fortified entrance (Beulé Gate) with two towers, which were built with material from destroyed choregic monuments.

Over the next two centuries and despite the difficulties, Athens slowly but surely recovered. Indicative of the new heyday is the creation of many large bath complexes, mainly in the east and south parts of the city. This flourishing anew was due exclusively to the existence and operation of the philosophical schools, where learned men from all over the Mediterranean taught and studied. To philosophical schools are attributed impressive architectural remains of opulent villas, which have been brought to light on the south slope of the Acropolis and the north slope of the Areopagus hill.

These schools, which had been founded in the fourth century BC by famous Greek philosophers, were pagan foundations in which Herakles, Hermes, the Nymphs and the Muses were worshipped. Despite the spread of Christianity, Athens remained a bastion of the old religion, much to the displeasure of the emperors in Constantinople. Finally, in AD 529, an edict of Justinian banned the teaching of philosophy and closed down the schools, thus ending a tradition going back over one thousand years. This move, as well as the

81 Athens. View from the southwest of the Roman Agora, an open flat square surrounded by stoas and shops. It was constructed in the second half of the 1st century BC, with gifts from Julius Caesar and Octavian Augustus. The octagonal building in the background is the Horologion of Andronikos Kyrrhestos, which housed in its interior the mechanism of a water-clock, while on the exterior was a sundial and on the top of the roof a weathervane. On the upper part of the sides are reliefs of personifications of the eight main winds, with their symbols.

81

raids by the Slavs in AD 582/3, dealt the final blow to the city, which lost its importance completely and gradually devolved into a small provincial town in the Byzantine Empire.

Today the capital of the Greek State, although sprawling and densely built up, Athens has succeeded in keeping some nuclei of archaeological interest, through which it is possible to gain an insight into its historical past [figs 58, 73, 76, 81, 90]. The Acropolis and the surrounding slopes, in combination with the Acropolis Museum [figs 83, 84], reflect the architectural and sculptural achievements of the Archaic and Classical periods, as well as the later uses of the sites. In the ancient Agora [figs 58, 76] we come into contact with the buildings and spaces where Athenian democracy was put into practice, while in the archaeological site and the museum of the Kerameikos, apart from the remnants of fortification walls, we see the splendid cemetery and the works of art in terracotta and marble, which accompanied the dead below and above ground. The new layout of the hills of Philopappos, the Pnyx and the Observatory, as well as the cleaning and enhancement of the ancient Koile Quarter, to the south of the church of St Demetrios Loumbardiaris, not only offer the opportunity of visiting important monuments but also of appreciating the original, natural picture of the ancient city. Another important site is the renovated grove of Plato's Academy, where some buildings of the ancient Gymnasium are preserved, while the very recent excavation of the palaestra of the Gymnasium of the Lykeion, in Rigillis Street, adds one further monument to the area. Last, the grand project of unification of the archaeological sites of Athens, as well as the exhibition of several of the finds unearthed most recently in the Metro stations have considerably enhanced the educative role of the city's antiquities and brought people into much more immediate contact with them. Thus, pieces of the superb aesthetic, artistic and technological achievements, and along with them some of the political, social and humanist messages of the illustrious past are brought into the present.

82

82 Athens. The monument of Philopappos was built on the summit of the hill of the Muses, by the rich prince who, having offered great benefactions to the city, was granted permission to found his mausoleum opposite the Acropolis. Shown here is the façade of the monument, with relief representations of Philopappos enthroned and upon a four-horse chariot (quadriga). The form and especially the position of the monument reflect the period of its creation (AD 114–116), and would have been unthinkable for even the most distinguished Athenian in Archaic and Classical times.

83, 84 Athens. View of the Parthenon Hall of the Acropolis Museum and of the access to it with the concordant coexistence of contemporary architecture and ancient monuments. The opening has been arranged so that part of the antiquities under the museum is visible. These are remains of a residential installation, as well as of workshops of the Late Roman and Early Byzantine periods, which were brought to light during the construction of the museum.

83

84

Sanctuaries of Attica

LYDIA PALAIOKRASSA-KOPITSA

In ancient Greece and specifically in Attica, where religion and history intertwined, the evolution of religion is articulated directly with the social and political organization. The inhabitants of Attica had a highly developed religious sentiment, as a result of which sanctuaries of gods and goddesses, as well as of secondary deities, heroes, mythological or historical figures, or heroized dead, were dispersed throughout the region (see Pausanias *Description of Greece* 1 17.1, 24.2–3; *Acts of the Apostles* 17.16). Cult practice, principal religious expression, was the means by which worshippers approached the divinity and was based on faith and related tenets and traditions. In Attica this practice seems to have had common elements for all inhabitants already from very ancient times, before the political unification of the region took place.

Cult was practised either officially by the State or the *demoi* [see map fig. 140], which also covered the expenses of the sanctuaries and the festivals [fig. 141], or by the devotees, who were free to communicate with the gods and to offer votive offerings or sacrifices in domestic shrines and public sanctuaries, individually or organized in various religious or social groups (*thiasotai*, *orgeones*, *eranistai*, etc., or *phratries*). Indicative of the above is the distinction made ([Aristotle], *Oec.* 1346 b 13–15) between public sanctuaries (*temene demosia*) and sanctuaries belonging to associations (*thiasotika*) or to phratries (*patriotika*). Practice of local cults was also the responsibility of various local organizations, such as the Tetrakomoi of Phaleron, a group of four *demoi* (Piraeus, Phaleron, Xypete, Thymaitadai) whose centre was the sanctuary of Herakles, the Tetrapolis of Marathon (Marathon, Oinoe, Trikorynthos and Probalinthos) or the League of Athena Pallenis.

Supreme religious authority was the *archon basileus*, the most senior of the officials of the Athenian State, responsible for the celebration of most of the sacrifices and festivals.

Without doubt, one of the principal sources for studying Attic worship is mythology, on which the Athenians had based their autochthony, with the hero-kings Kekrops [fig. 86] and Erechtheus (Homer, *Iliad* II 547) as the dominant figures. Some sanctuaries are linked by textual tradition with

85

85 Athens. Part of an inscription which in Antiquity was placed in the Royal (Basileios) Stoa of the Agora. It included the code of sacrifices, in which Solon's calendar of sacrifices was recorded and reformed in the late 5th century BC. The task of recording and reforming this calendar had been entrusted among others to Nikomachos. Athens, Museum of the Ancient Agora.

86 Athens, Acropolis. Parthenon, west pediment (438–432 BC). Complex of the mythical autochthonous first king of Athens, Kekrops, with one of his three daughters (Pandrosos). Kekrops has a serpent's tail. The subject of the sculpted decoration on the west pediment was the dispute between Athena and Poseidon over possession of the land of Attica. Athens, Acropolis Museum.

mythical heroes of Attica, such as the sanctuary on the acropolis of Lamptrai, dedicated to the cult of the Athenian king Kranaos, or the sanctuary of Prasiai, where the *par excellence* god of the Ionians, Apollo, was worshipped and which was founded on the burial spot of Kekrops' son Erysichthon. Associated with the Trojan cycle is the sanctuary of Artemis at Brauron, the central figure in whose cult was Iphigeneia, who was believed to have been the first priestess of the goddess. Homer and the Homeric Hymns generally preserve much information on the mythological past of Attica and its cults.

Thucydides (2.15) too records significant testimony on the existence of the very ancient sanctuaries of Zeus Olympios, Apollo Pythios, Gaia, Dionysos *en Limnais*, and other deities, to the south of the Acropolis. This information is verified by the archaeological evidence from the area of the River Ilissos, where, in addition to the aforesaid sanctuaries, there were also the sanctuaries of Kronos and Rhea, of Apollo Delphinios, Artemis, Zeus Meilichios, Aphrodite, Pan, Kodros (last mythical king of Athens), who was worshipped jointly with Neleus and Basile, deities of the Underworld, of Athena Pallas and of Herakles, Palaimon and Pankrates. Other texts take the existence of cults back to most ancient times (e.g. of Zeus Polieus on the Acropolis or of Apollo Pythios on its north slope).

There is a great deal of information on Athenian worship in the calendar of sacrifices, which was said to have been compiled by the archon and legislator Solon in the early sixth century BC and constituted the last part of his Laws, parts of which are preserved in ancient Greek texts [fig. 85].

86

87

87 Athens. Frieze consisting of two stone blocks, incorporated in second use in the Middle Byzantine church of St Eleutherios, adjacent to the Greek Orthodox cathedral of Athens. The frieze is particularly important for our understanding of the Attic festive calendar, because it carries a relief representation of the Attic months, personified as youths or men, accompanied in some cases by gods or by figures characteristic of the main festivals, or personifications of concepts, as well as by symbols of the zodiac cycle. The months Gamelion and Anthesterion have been destroyed, as has the ship of the Panathenaia, which was represented together with the personification of the procession and the month Hekatombaion. Possibly 1st century BC.

Testimonies on religious life in Attica are also drawn from other literary sources, mainly the traveller Pausanias or the Atthidographers, writers (4th– early 3rd century BC) narrating Athenian history, who record many myths and details about various cults, as well as from inscriptions, which preserve decisions concerning the practice of State *worship*, sacred laws, lists of the objects in the possession of the sanctuaries and calendars of sacrifices. The last contain much information on the cultic activity of the inhabitants of Attica, which took place in the areas of their home, that consisted the Kleisthenian *demoi*. The contribution of iconography is particularly significant too for understanding religious life in Attica [fig. 87].

The earliest signs of human presence at sanctuary sites in Attica during prehistoric times are encountered in the sanctuaries of Zeus on the summit of Hymettos and of Parnes, of Artemis Mounichia in Piraeus, of Poseidon on Cape Sounion, of Apollo Delios at Prasiai and of Demeter at Eleusis. However, it is not certain that these signs are related to worship. Nor does present evidence document the early practice of cult in the subsequently most important sanctuary in Attica, that of Athena on the Acropolis of Athens [fig. 90], notwithstanding the testimonies of tradition, which associate worship with the mythical kings of the city. A *locus sanctus* with *eschara* on the west side of the bastion of the west Mycenaean entrance to the Acropolis and of the later tower of the temple of Athena Nike [fig. 88], which was preserved when the Cyclopean wall was built, bears witness to the existence of some early cult, but with no other evidence (heroon of the mythical king Aegeus, Gate shrine or of Athena Pylatis?).

The change in social and political organization during the Geometric period (9th–8th century BC) can be detected in the appearance of large organized sanctuaries in Athens, as well as in the *chora*, that is, the rural territory of Attica. Quite early signs of the practice of cult, already from the tenth century BC, exist in the sanctuaries of Zeus on Hymettos and Parnes, in the sanctuary of Artemis Mounichia and in the sanctuary of Kronos in the environs of the River Ilissos. In other cases, the nature of the deities for whom later indications of worship survive, confirms the early practice of cult, such

88

88 Athens, Acropolis. The Ionic temple of Athena Nike (430–420 BC), built on top of the tower that incorporated the bastion of the Mycenaean fortification. The pediments and the frieze bore sculpted decoration in which historical events were represented for the first time (battles of Greeks "against those of their race and those not of their race", as attested by Pausanias).

89 Athens. Bronze figurine of a naked warrior, which adorned the handle of a bronze tripod, votive offering on the Acropolis of Athens. Early 7th century BC. Athens, National Archaeological Museum.

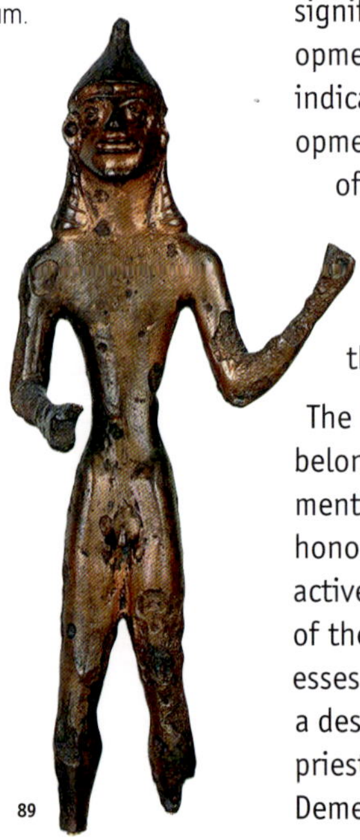

89

as in the case of various fertility-chthonic deities (Demeter Chloe, Ge Kourotrophos and Olympia, and others).

Religious activity intensified during Geometric times, particularly in the eighth century BC, as is ascertained from the votive offerings of devotees in most sanctuaries that flourished later, in Archaic and Classical times, such as the sanctuaries of Athena on the Acropolis [fig. 89], of Zeus on Hymettos and Parnes, of Demeter at Eleusis, of Artemis at Mounichia and Brauron, of Apollo Delphinios near the Ilissos and Delios at Prasiai. There was a proliferation of organized sanctuaries and a flourishing of hero cult.

It is generally accepted that towards the end of the eighth and primarily during the seventh century BC, a more intense religious activity is observed in Attica, which is documented by the large concentration of offerings in cult places. This concentration attests to the organization of the sanctuaries and of the collective cult practices, the grouping of people of dissimilar social strata and of their devotion to a particular cult, to a common religious life, as is ascertained from the diversity of votive offerings within the same sanctuary. Ascertained too is a certain differentiation in the confrontation of the divine, in relation to the previous period, manifested, for example, in the expression of the worshippers' own personal identity and the individual's attempt at a direct communication with the deity, which the appearance of inscribed sherds in the sanctuary of Zeus on Hymettos is considered to express [fig. 96].

The observed burgeoning of religious life of Attica in this period reveals a significant watershed in worship, which has been correlated with the development of the city-state, under the aegis of the nobles (*Eupatridai*). Also indicative of the existence of an organized religious community is the development of the sanctuary of the patron goddess Athena Polias, at the centre of Athens, on the Acropolis, in conjunction with the sanctuary of Zeus Polieus, patron too of the institutions of the *polis*. The flourishing of the sanctuaries in the Attic *chora*, such as at Eleusis, Sounion, Mounichia, Brauron, Halai Araphenides and Prasiai, also presupposes the organization of the inhabitants of the settlements of the later *demoi*.

The important place held by the *gene*, the clans to which the Athenians belonged on the basis of their origin, is considered to be a survival of elements of aristocracy in the religious life of Athens in later times. The clans honoured their own eponymous heroes-ancestors, but also participated actively in the cult practices of the Athenians, with specific duties. To many of these the State had entrusted the hereditary office of priests or priestesses of the various gods. The *hierophantes* of the Eleusinian Mysteries was a descendant of the Eumolpidai clan, the priestess of Athena Polias and the priest of Poseidon Erechtheus from the Eteoboutadai, the priestess of Demeter and Kore from the Philleidai. Other clans, such as the Kerykes [fig.

90 Athens. Aerial photograph of the Acropolis and the area of the River Ilissos, from the northwest. Both areas were prominent centres of worship in Antiquity as well as in Early Christian times. The Acropolis hosted the religious centre of the city, with the worship of its patron goddess Athena, while the Ilissos area was scattered with important sanctuaries. Visible on the Sacred Rock are the North Wall built by Themistocles, the Propylaia, the Parthenon, the Erechtheion and, between them, the foundations for the Archaios Neos, while on the north slope are caves, most of them devoted to cult [fig. 21]. In the background extends the area of the Ilissos, in which can be seen the arch erected by the Athenians to honour Emperor Hadrian and the ruins of the temple of Zeus Olympios.

90

104], the Praxiergidai, the Lykomidai, the Bouzygai or the Salaminioi were responsible for organizing specific festivals or cult events.

Religious activity during the seventh century BC continued at the same sites, although new ones also appeared, such as in the area of Athens (the sanctuary of Nymphe, deity of marriage, south of the Acropolis, the Eleusinion, the sanctuary of the Nymphs at Pnyx), at Lathureza, Varkiza, Thorikos, Sounion, Merenda (anc. Myrrhinous) and Prophitis Ilias at Koropi.

Places of worship can now be distinguished into sanctuaries in the *Asty* and sanctuaries in the Attic *chora*, the most important of which later evolved into cult centres of the *demoi*, of local or wider ambit, and into sanctuaries in isolated places. In addition to the above, there is evidence too of small domestic shrines. A significant factor in the choice of a sanctuary site was the natural environment.

At the centre of Athens, on the Rock of the Acropolis, was the sanctuary of the protectress of the city Athena, the only sanctuary, it seems, in which there was a monumental arrangement prior to the sixth century BC, with the existence at least of the temple of Athena Polias, on the site of the Mycenaean palace, of the "rich temple" or the "well-built house of Erechtheus", as it is called by Homer (*Iliad* II 549, *Odyssey* vii 81). It is accepted by scholarship today that at least two small temples existed in the seventh century BC. In its heyday, particularly from the end of the eighth century BC onwards, the sanctuary's fame spread beyond the boundaries of Attica and approached that of the panhellenic sanctuaries.

In the Attic countryside there were sanctuaries, either independent or incorporated in settlements, that hosted important cults. The sanctuaries of the rural settlements were the religious centres of the local societies, but many also attracted worshippers from all over Attica and their festivals were included in official State cult. In several cases the festivals included a splendid procession that set off from the *Asty*, usually from the "common hearth" in the Prytaneion or the Pompeion in the Kerameikos [fig. 58], and terminated at the sanctuaries.

Another sanctuary belonging to the category of sanctuaries of settlements in the Attic *chora* is that of Eleusis [figs 126–128], founded in the fertile Thriasion

91 Piraeus, sanctuary of Artemis Mounichia. Sherd of a small krater (krateriskos), with depiction of a running arktos. These vases of standardized shape and decoration were used in cult and are dated to the late 6th and the early 5th century BC. They carry mainly black-figure representations of girls, naked or clothed, walking or dancing, in front of altars or palm trees, holding wreaths, ribbons, torches or rattles (krotala). In rare cases fawns are depicted, the sacred animals of the goddess. The girls are identified as the arktoi. Piraeus Archaeological Museum.

92 Brauron, sanctuary of Artemis. Marble statuette of a little girl holding a rabbit in the folds of her himation. This was a votive offering in the sanctuary of Artemis. Second half of 4th century BC. Earlier scholars identified the statuettes of girls from Brauron as the arktoi (= bears), young Athenian maidens who participated in the rite of passage of the arkteia. Brauron Archaeological Museum.

93 Piraeus, sanctuary of Artemis Mounichia. Krateriskos with high foot depicting an altar and a palm tree. Piraeus Archaeological Museum.

94 Brauron. Aerial view of the sanctuary of Artemis. The earliest finds date back to the founding of the sanctuary in the 9th century BC. The surviving Doric temple of poros stone (in the middle of the lower part of the photograph) was built upon a manmade terrace in the first half of the 5th century BC, beside a spring from which the River Erasinos flows. The temple was distyle in antis, with prodomos and adyton, while the cella was three-aisled. Towards the end of the 5th century BC, a Π-shaped stoa was built, enclosing a court in front of the temple. In nine of the eleven rooms at the rear of the stoa were couches and tables, perhaps dining rooms or accommodation for the ritual meals that took place during the festival of the goddess. East of the chapel of St George, which is thought to have been built on earlier constructions, to the right of the temple, in a narrow passage in the rock — probably once a cave — a small temple-shaped building was erected (Heroon of Iphigeneia?). The cult of Artemis at Brauron was parallel to her cult at Mounichia and was addressed to the goddess as protectress of nature, children, women, marriage and family life. It was related directly to coming of age, fertility and successful childbearing.

93

94

95

plain. It was probably local in character but its fame quickly spread beyond the boundaries of the local society and acquired panhellenic glory. This is the second sanctuary in Attica at which building activity is documented already from the eighth century BC.

Other sanctuaries were founded in coastal regions, such as the sanctuary of Artemis Mounichia [figs 91, 93], of Aphrodite on Cape Kolias (pres. Agios Kosmas), the sanctuaries of Poseidon and Athena on Cape Sounion [figs 111, 112], of Apollo at Prasiai (pres. Porto Rafti) and Zoster (pres. Vouliagmeni: figs 156, 157) and the sanctuary of Artemis Tauropolos at Halai Araphenides (pres. Loutsa), or close to a river or a spring, such as the sanctuary of Artemis at Brauron [fig. 94]. Of significance in the selection of the site for the sanctuaries at Mounichia, Sounion and Prasiai was surely their prominent location and their proximity to the harbours. Here gathered mariners and merchants, to whom the wealth of votive offerings is largely due.

In the two sanctuaries of Artemis, at Brauron and Mounichia, little girls were secluded, in order to abandon the "wild" nature of childhood and, reborn, to spend their adolescence and become accepted as adults in civilized society [fig. 92]. It is characteristic that all the sanctuaries dedicated to deities whose cult included similar rites of passage are isolated outside cities, in the far reaches (*eschaties*). These cults, which enjoyed a particular heyday during the seventh, fifth and fourth centuries BC, were directly related to social organization.

In addition to the large sanctuaries, smaller and poorer sanctuaries existed in the various *demoi*, incorporated in the urban tissue of the settlements [figs 158, 167], which usually comprised a walled precinct (*peribolos*), a small temple and an altar. Inscriptions found at sanctuary sites have enabled the identification of the deity worshipped, as in the small sanctuary excavated recently at Merenda (anc. Myrrhinous), which was dedicated to Zeus Phratrios.

Rural sanctuaries were founded either in connection with farming settlements, such as the sanctuary at Lathureza in Vari, which dates from the late eighth century BC and was dedicated probably dedicated to a female chthonic deity, or on hills or mountain tops, which continued the tradition

96

95 Sounion. Terracotta pinax from the peribolos in the sanctuary of Athena at Sounion **[fig. 140]**, where a hero (Phrontis?) with nautical qualities is believed to have been worshipped. Attributed to the so-called Analatos Painter, it is dated *ca* 700 BC. Depicted is part of a ship with helmsman and hoplites. Athens, National Archaeological Museum.

96 Sherds of Attic vases inscribed with the names of the dedicators or of the god (Zeus Ombrios and Semeios), from the sanctuary on the summit of Mt Hymettos. The earliest are dated to the first half of 7th century BC. Among the earliest surviving examples of script in Attica. Athens, Museum of the Ancient Agora.

97, 98 Athens, Acropolis. Korai statues, votive offerings of wealthy Athenians to the goddess Athena, represent maidens dressed in luxurious garments and jewellery, the details of which were painted. They are attired usually in a chiton and an Ionic himation draped obliquely, and held diverse offerings. It is estimated that over two hundred such statues stood on the Acropolis from around 560 BC onwards, which date coincides with the celebration of the first re-organized Great Panathenaia, in 566/5 BC. Various views have been expressed on the reasons for their dedication, which was intended to invoke the goddess's favour, delight and satisfaction. They are considered to have been offered in commemoration of some office conferred on the girls, and to be images of Arrephoroi, priestesses or even Athena herself.

97 The Peplophoros. Pentelic marble. *Ca* 530 BC. The kore wears a chiton and a peplos girdled at the waist. The statue originally had lavish painted decoration, a metal wreath on the head and earrings. It is considered to be the work of a sculptor to whom the so-called Rampin Horseman and other Archaic sculptures have been attributed. Distinguished by the harmony, nobility and spirituality which creations of the Attic workshop emanate. Athens, Acropolis Museum.

98 The earliest kore from the Acropolis. Pentelic marble. 570/60 BC. She wears a chiton girdled at the waist and a long himation that falls from the shoulders, while around her neck is a necklace. In her right hand she holds a wreath, and in the left, bent onto the chest, a pomegranate. Athens, Acropolis Museum.

97

98

99 Athens, Acropolis. Three sculptural groups in poros stone, which have been recomposed from many fragments, have been attributed to the west pediment of the Hekatompedon. At the centre of the composition there was perhaps the group of two lions attacking a bull; on the right the three-bodied daemon, possibly Nereus, with three human torsos in the upper part and three coiling serpent tails in the lower; on the left a group of Herakles struggling with Triton, with Nereus watching from the right. In the cunei of the pediment were two big snakes. The figures were embellished with elaborate painted decoration. Athens, Acropolis Museum.

of the peak sanctuaries of prehistoric times. Observed in these sanctuaries, in the majority of which worship of Zeus is confirmed, is a considerable increase in the number of votive offerings from the Late Geometric period. Typical is the case of the sanctuary of Zeus on the summit of Mount Hymettos [fig. 96]. This, together with that on the Karabola peak of Mount Parnes, are the earliest and the most important sancturies of the category, in which Zeus was worshipped as god of the weather phenomena and probably in his wider hypostasis as protector of the heavenly world of agriculture and soil fertility, as well as of society, and as fiduciary of justice. There are similar cases of sanctuaries on the top of Prophitis Ilias at Koropi, at Argrieliki in the area of Marathon, on Keratovouni at Keratea, on Mount Pani, at Kiafa Thiti, at Varkiza and at Tourkovouni, most of which flourished during the seventh century BC but declined during the sixth. The rural population of the surrounding areas gathered in these sanctuaries. However, the cases of the two sanctuaries of Zeus, on Hymettos and Parnes, and possibly the sanctuary at Kiafa Thiti, were different, since these seem to have transcended the boundaries of the surrounding rural area. The expansion of cults in the *chora* of Attica was influenced more generally by the development of agriculture in the second half of the eighth century BC.

Small rural sanctuaries, in which the deities worshipped are difficult to identify, have been excavated all over Attica. Founded beside road arteries, these are of more or less the same form as the small urban sanctuaries.

100

Particularly widespread in Attica was hero cult, the spread of which from the late eighth century BC reflects the organization of Attic society in clans (*gene*), from the mythical heroes-founders of which the local cults were shaped.

Hero cult is documented in the area of the Athenian Agora, in earlier tombs, as well as in the Attic *chora*, where isolated practice of cult was attested in the *dromos* of Mycenaean tholos tombs in the area of ancient Acharnai (Lykotrypa at Menidi), Thorikos [fig. 14] and Alyki at Voula. This phenomenon has been much discussed by scholars and has been correlated with the so-called internal colonization of Attica, that is the settlement of people in rural areas of the Attic *chora* during the Late Geometric period. However, the material from the sites is related more to the practice of this cult by the aristocracy of the time and its effort to emphasize its superior origin, to enhance its status and to link itself to the heroic ancestral past.

In very few cases is it possible to correlate the archaeological data with heroic figures of myth, as at Sounion with Menelaos' helmsman Phrontis [fig. 95], who died on returning from Troy and was buried on the cape.

In later times too, Attic *demoi* worshipped local heroes, many of whom provided ancestral identity and autochthony for the *demotai* and their name for the *demos*, such as the hero Thorikos to Thorikos, Marathos or Marathon to Marathon. Lesser heroes also existed, linked with local traditions, as well as heroic figures of myth, which the State had elevated to symbols, for reasons of propaganda. The most important examples are Herakles, whom the Peisistratids promoted, and Theseus [fig. 22], the hero *par excellence* of the

100 Panathenaic amphora, front. Attributed to the Kleophrades Painter. *Ca* 490 BC. Leiden, Rijksmuseum van Oudheden. Panathenaic amphorae were of large size, of standardized shape and had black-figure decoration. Depicted on the front is Athena Promachos, fully armed, framed by two columns and accompanied by the inscription: ΤΩΝ ΑΘΗΝΗΘΕΝ ΑΘΛΩΝ (of the games in Athens). Represented in the back is the contest in which the amphora's recipient was victor. Each vase held about 38 kilos of olive oil. The dating of the earliest surviving Panathenaic amphora coincides more or less with the date of celebration of the first re-organized Great Panathenaia, in 566/5 BC. These amphorae continued to be produced until the early 4th century AD. The number of amphorae awarded to each winner depended on the importance of the contest and was up to a maximum of 140, in the case of chariot races.

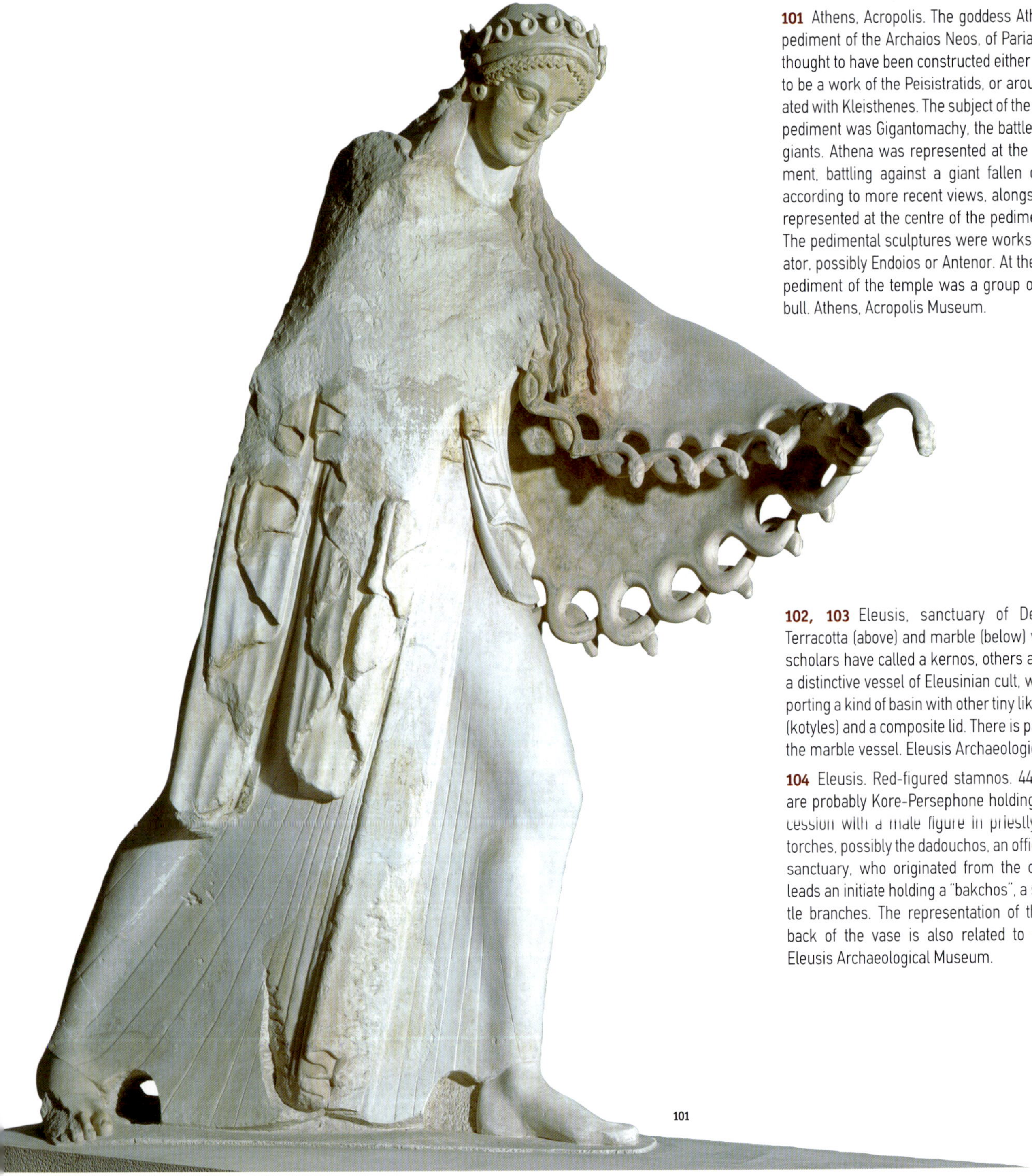

101

101 Athens, Acropolis. The goddess Athena from the east pediment of the Archaios Neos, of Parian marble, which is thought to have been constructed either around 525 BC and to be a work of the Peisistratids, or around 510 BC, associated with Kleisthenes. The subject of the composition on the pediment was Gigantomachy, the battle between gods and giants. Athena was represented at the centre of the pediment, battling against a giant fallen on the ground, or, according to more recent views, alongside Zeus, who was represented at the centre of the pediment, upon a chariot. The pedimental sculptures were works of an inspired creator, possibly Endoios or Antenor. At the centre of the west pediment of the temple was a group of a lion attacking a bull. Athens, Acropolis Museum.

102, 103 Eleusis, sanctuary of Demeter and Kore. Terracotta (above) and marble (below) vessel, which some scholars have called a kernos, others a plemochoe. This is a distinctive vessel of Eleusinian cult, with a high foot supporting a kind of basin with other tiny like vessels on the rim (kotyles) and a composite lid. There is painted decoration on the marble vessel. Eleusis Archaeological Museum.

104 Eleusis. Red-figured stamnos. 440–435 BC. Depicted are probably Kore-Persephone holding a torch and a procession with a male figure in priestly garb, holding two torches, possibly the dadouchos, an official in the Eleusinian sanctuary, who originated from the clan of Kerykes. He leads an initiate holding a "bakchos", a sheaf of bound myrtle branches. The representation of three figures on the back of the vase is also related to the Eleusinian cult. Eleusis Archaeological Museum.

Athenian Democracy, symbol of Athenian heroism and glory, whose alleged bones were translated with honours to Athens, after the conquest of Skyros by Kimon in 476/5 BC. They were placed in the sanctuary dedicated to him in the city centre, while the Theseia festival was established to commemorate him. Other Athenian festivals were also associated with the myth of Theseus, such as the Synoikia, the Kybernesia, the Oschophoria and the Pyanepsia.

The first major building works in the sanctuaries of Attica were undertaken by the tyrant Peisistratos and his sons, under whose rule (561–510 BC) Athens enjoyed a veritable building boom. It was then that the first monumental temples of the *polis* and the *asty*, as well as of the countryside, were built, such as the first temples of Athena Pallenis and Sounias, of Artemis at Brauron and of Nemesis at Rhamnous.

Peisistratos is accredited too with reorganizing the festival of the Panathenaia, the greatest and most glorious of the city, which according to textual sources was instituted in the archonship of Hippokleides, in 566/5 BC. The Great Panathenaia, which achieved panhellenic fame, were celebrated every four years and included athletic games (gymnastic, equestrian and *apobatikoi* mounting and dismounting chariots contests), music contests, a nocturnal vigil (*pannychis*), a torch race (*lampadedromia*), the procession that ended at the temple of Athena Polias where the peplos was presented to the goddess, and the sacrifice of 100 oxen (*hecatomb*). Hipparchos is said to have also introduced the recitation of the Homeric epics. Only Athenian citizens were permitted to participate in the games associated with Athenian traditions. The victor's prize in many contests was olive oil, held in the famous Panathenaic amphorae [fig. 100].

The Acropolis was by now the most splendid religious centre in Attica. Here was built the stone peripteral temple of Athena Polias, south of the later Erechtheion, while the sanctuary was adorned with a host of statues, opulent *ex-votos* of wealthy Athenians to the goddess. These statues, mainly of korai [figs 65, 97, 98], were found inside pits and deposits which the archaeologists called the "Persian *apothetai*" (apothetis-pit), in which they had been placed after the destruction of Athens by the Persians in 480 BC. The Acropolis also acquired a monumental entrance on its west side, with the construction of a ramp that facilitated the ascent of worshippers to the rock, and particularly of the Panathenaic procession. Furthermore, in the last quarter of the sixth century BC, rural cults were transferred to the city, for political reasons. A sanctuary of Artemis Brauronia [fig. 67] was founded on the southwest side of the rock of the Acropolis, while the sanctuary of Dionysos, whose cult had been brought from the city of Eleutherai on the Attic-Boeotian border, was founded on the south slope. In this latter sanc-

102

103

104

105

105, 107 Athens, Acropolis. Blocks from the east side of the Parthenon frieze. Represented at the centre of this side [fig. 105] are two girls carrying stools and a footstool, a female figure, probably the priestess of Athena, and a male figure (archon basileus, priest?) receiving the peplos from a child. The scene of handing over the peplos is framed left by Zeus enthroned and Hera, and right by Athena and Hephaistos. London, British Museum.

Right [fig. 107], block with the figures of Poseidon, Apollo and Artemis. Athens, Acropolis Museum. The Parthenon frieze, of overall length 160 m, comprised 115 blocks carrying a relief representation of the procession of the Great Panathenaia, with 192 figures. Its execution involved the collaboration of many artists, under the guidance of the inspirer of the work, Pheidias. The procession was the climax of the festival, celebrated on the birthday of the goddess, the 28th day of the month of Hekatombaion (about mid-August). The festival of Athena, the Panathenaia, was celebrated annually in this month, whereas the Great Panathenaia were celebrated every four years. At the Great Panathenaia the peplos, embroidered with scenes of Gigantomachy, was delivered to the goddess. Preparations for the procession took place in the Pompeion, from where it departed to progress in the direction of the Acropolis, via the Panathenaic Way [fig. 58]. The peplos was hoisted on the mast of the Panathenaic ship. It was taken down from the mast at the foot of the Acropolis, at the Eleusinion, and then handed over to the priest, who deposited it at the wooden cult statue (xoanon) of Athena Polias in the Archaios Neos. A sacrifice of one hundred oxen (hecatomb) was made on the altar of the goddess. The procession on the frieze starts at the southwest corner of the temple and moves towards the east side in two branches. Represented on the west frieze is the preparation and departure of the horsemen. On the north and south sides parade horsemen with quadrigae and apobatai, who mount and dismount the chariots, in full armour. Behind them, on foot, are officials, youths and maidens holding various ritual vessels [fig. 70], young men driving animals to sacrifice, musicians and the ten eponymous heroes, representatives of the ten tribes of Attica, who frame the

106

assembly of the Olympian gods. The gods are arranged in two groups on either side of the central scene of the handing over of the peplos. According to some interpretations of the representation, it illustrates the first procession of the Panathenaia, which was established by Erichthonios, or the first procession after 480 BC. It has been argued too that the 192 figures on the frieze represent the 192 who fell in the battle of Marathon, and that on the south side participants are organized in ten groups corresponding to the ten tribes of Kleisthenes' reforms, while on the north side they are in twelve groups, corresponding to the twelve pre-Kleisthenian phratries.

106 Modern representation of the chryselephantine statue of Athena Parthenos, after the descriptions in the ancient sources and the few copies in marble, mainly of Roman times. The original work by Pheidias was placed in the cella of the Parthenon in 438 BC. There was rich decoration in relief on the helmet, the shield, the thick soles of the footwear and the base of the statue. On the inside of the shield there was a painted representation. Toronto, Royal Ontario Museum.

107

108 Eleusis. The large Eleusinian relief. 440–430 BC. Represented on the left is Demeter, wearing a peplos and holding a sceptre, handing over to a young man, possibly Triptolemos, an ear of wheat, so that he can teach men how to cultivate cereals. On the right is Kore-Persephone, in chiton and himation, holding a torch. Athens, National Archaeological Museum.

tuary were celebrated the Great or *En astei* (city) Dionysia, one of the most important festivals of Athens, the demands of the celebration of which led shortly after 500 BC to the creation of the earliest theatre. The festival included one or possibly two processions, sacrifices, choric singing and dancing, as well as phallic parading (*phallophoria*), a revel (*komos*), drama [fig. 113] and dithyramb competitions. Drama competitions had also been included in the Lenaia, the festival for Dionysos Lenaios.

Despite the preservation of the foundations of the peripteral temple of Athena Polias to the south of Erechtheion, and of a large number of architectural members and sculptures, mainly pedimental, from various sixth-century BC buildings on the Acropolis, the aspect of the Sacred Rock in this period remains relatively vague. Scholars disagree as to how many and to which temples the surviving architectural members should be attributed [figs 69, 90]. There are two basic views regarding the temples of Athena on the Sacred Rock during the sixth century BC: 1) there were two temples, the one known in the sources as the "Old Temple" (*Archaios Neos* or *Naos o en polei*), dedicated to Athena Polias, whose cult was the most important in the city, and the other the so-called *Hekatompedos Neos*, which was possibly located slightly north of the Periclean Parthenon, dedicated to Athena Parthenos/Pallas, and 2) there was one temple with two building phases, that is there was only the *Archaios Neos* [fig. 101].

108

Athena was worshipped also as Nike (Victory), to the south of the central entrance to the Acropolis, where a bastion of the Mycenaean Cyclopean wall [fig. 88] pre-existed and later the Classical temple was built, as is confirmed by the dedication of an inscribed altar by an Athenian named Patrokles, shortly before the mid-sixth century BC.

Surviving architectural sculptures further document the existence of smaller buildings, which research has identified with the *oikemata* known from the sources. Most scholars consider that these were treasuries (*thesauroi*), that is, edifices for the safekeeping of precious objects of the sanctuary. The site of only one is known, below the Pinakotheke, the north wing of the Mnesiklean Propylaia.

Dominant in the subjects of the sixth-century BC pedimental sculptures from the Acropolis is the figure of Herakles [fig. 99], whose significance for the tyrants has been mentioned above, while towards the end of the century the figure of majestic and fully-armed Athena appears, waging battle against the Giants [fig. 101].

Among the ambitions of the tyrants was to build on the banks of the Ilissos the largest temple in Athens and indeed in the whole of

109

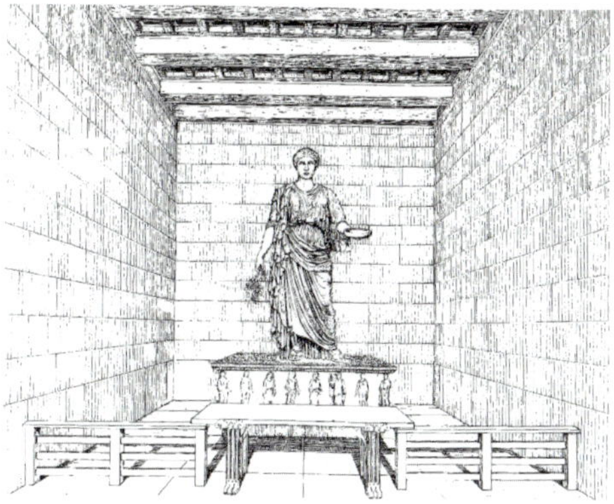

110

109, 110 Rhamnous. In the area of a fort in Attica, at Rhamnous **[fig. 145]**, there was an important sanctuary dedicated to Nemesis, a deity of chthonic nature, protectress of balance, rural order and measure, punisher of hybris, excess and arrogance. So, for obvious reasons, the sanctuary, which was the religious centre of the demos, acquired special significance after the Persian Wars. Also worshipped hereabouts were Themis, Aristomachos and, later, Amphiaraos, Dionysos, Hermes, Apollo, Zeus Soter and Athena Soteira, Demeter and Kore, Kybele (Agdistis), Aphrodite, the hero Neanias, the Egyptian deities and other secondary divinities.

The sanctuary of Nemesis, in which cult practices are confirmed from the early 6th century BC, occupied a terrace. The earliest temple was built in the opening decades of the 6th century BC, while at the end of the century a second poros temple in the Doric order was erected, which was destroyed most probably by the Persians. After 480 BC a third temple of the goddess was constructed, known as polygonal or temple of Themis, which was preserved as a treasury (thesauros) until the early 4th century AD, when the sanctuary ceased to operate. After the mid-5th century BC, construction of the large peripteral temple of Nemesis, in Pentelic marble, commenced next to the above temple. This remained unfinished, most probably because of the outbreak of the Peloponnesian War. The Parian marble cult statue of the goddess was a work by Pheidias' pupil Agorakritos and has been recomposed by Professor G. Despinis from hundreds of fragments (above). The sanctuary included also the altar, a stoa with wooden columns and a fountain of the second half of the 5th century BC.

The Nemesia, the festival of the goddess, were celebrated with a sacrifice, athletic games and a torch race (lampadedromia). During the Lenaia festival in honour of Dionysos, celebrated in the god's sanctuary at Rhamnous, drama competitions were held in the theatre of the demos.

111

Hellas, after the model of the monumental temples of the East. This project was not completed until many centuries later. The temple, dipteral, most probably in the Doric order, almost double the size of its early Archaic predecessor, was dedicated to Zeus Olympios [fig. 90]. The tyrants also showed interest in the sanctuary of Apollo Pythios [figs 26, 27], in the same area. Tradition has it (Hesychius *Lexicon* s.v. *en Pythio chesai* ("ἐν Πυθίῳ χέσαι") that they tried to build a new temple of the god but came up against the resistance of the Athenians.

Under Peisistratos the Younger (522/1 BC) the Altar of the Twelve Gods was founded in the northwest corner of the Agora, along the west side of which small temples were built to house the cults of Zeus, Apollo Patroos and possibly the Mother of the Gods. Towards the end of the sixth century BC, for political reasons the sanctuary of the Aeginetan hero Aiakos was built in an honorary position in the Agora, when relations between the two cities, Aegina and Athens, were particularly tense.

At Eleusis [figs 126–128] the sanctuary was reorganized and a new Telesterion was constructed shortly after the mid-sixth century BC.

Tradition attributes to Peisistratos the earliest temple of Artemis at Brauron. The tyrants' interest in their place of origin, from the population of which they drew their support, is well known. Some smaller Archaic sanctuaries in the Mesogaia, such as the temples at Loutsa and at Prophitis Ilias on Hymettos, are also possibly associated with the Peisistratids.

After the fall of the tyranny, Kleisthenes' reforms seem to have marked a turning point in the religious life of the Athenians, in which, of the agents of Kleisthenes' political organizationthe *demoi*, the *trittyes* and the tribes (*phyles*), the *demoi* held prominent place. At a local level they had their own sanctuaries, often with theatres [fig. 150] in which drama contests were held, and their own sacrificial calendars [fig. 141], the keeping of which was the responsibility of the *demarchos*. However, at the official State festivals representation of the people of Attica was based on the tribes. The handling of many religious affairs, such as the finances of the sanctuaries or even, in some cases, the priesthood, was now controlled also by the *Ekklesia* of the *demos* and the *Boule*. Concurrently, ancient traditions relating to social or political organization were kept, such as the Apatouria festival, at which the children were registered in the phratries, equivalent to today's registering in the municipal roll, which was accompanied by sacrifice to Zeus Phratrios and Athena Phratria. The phratries also honoured Apollo Patroos, while each one had in addition its own patron deities or heroes.

Apart from the Panathenaia and other official festivals of the Athenians, such as the Eleusinian Mysteries [figs 102–104, 108, 126–128], the Diipolia, Diasia, Thargelia, Anthesteria, the *En astei* or Great and the *Kat' agrous*

111 The marble kouros of Sounion. *Ca* 600 BC. One of the earliest kouros statues from the Attic workshop. A colossal creation (h. 3.05 m) which had been dedicated in the sanctuary of Poseidon at Sounion, where it was found together with fragments of other kouroi, inside a deposit (apothetes). The kouros is illustrated here with its old restorations. Athens, National Archaeological Museum.

112 Sounion, temple of Poseidon. Evidence referring to the rich religious life of the inhabitants of the demos is drawn from inscriptions of the Salaminioi clan, which held an important place in general in the religious life of Athens. The religious centre of the demos consisted of the sanctuaries of Poseidon and Athena on the cape **[fig. 144]**, where worship flourished from the 7th century BC onward. The earliest reference to Sounion as a sanctuary is encountered in Homer (Odyssey iii 278). The temple was built of Agrileza marble, on the southernmost tip of the headland, in 444–440 BC, and succeeded the unfinished temple (building had commenced in 490 BC) destroyed by the Persians. The sacred precinct (temenos) of Poseidon was delimited by a built circuit wall (peribolos) and was entered through a monumental propylon in the north side. In the neighbouring sanctuary of Athena there is evidence, in an elliptical enclosure, of the cult of a hero, already in the 7th century BC. Of nautical character, he has been identified with Phrontis, helmsman of Menelaos **[fig. 95]**. A small and simple prostyle cella in the Doric order is dated either to the first half of the 6th century BC, according to one view, or to the second half of the 5th century BC, according to another, and was dedicated to Athena or Artemis. The bigger temple, in the Ionic order, of the mid-5th century BC, had a colonnade on the east and south sides, and was dedicated to Athena. Every four years, a festival was held at Sounion, with contests between warships, to which the Athenians came by ship (theorida naun/ θεωρίδα ναῦν) from the Piraeus.

112

113 Piraeus. Marble relief. *Ca* 400 BC. It had been dedicated to Dionysos, represented reclining on a couch holding a phiale and a rhyton, by a company of actors, after a performance, possibly of the Bacchae by Euripides, as the drums and masks held by the actors suggest. The scene illustrates iconographically the importance of drama in the worship of Dionysos all over Attica. Athens, National Archaeological Museum.

114 Athens. The sanctuary and the theatre of Dionysos, on the south slope of the Acropolis. During the archonship of Lykourgos (336–324 BC) a peribolos was built around the sanctuary and a Doric stoa at the rear of the skene of the theatre, the cavea of which was enlarged and built in stone.

113

114

115

115 Piraeus. Marble votive relief from the Asklepieion in the Piraeus. Represented is Asklepios accompanied by his daughter Hygeia, curing a patient lying on a bed. On the left are the sick woman's family and probably the dedicator herself. Late 5th century BC. Piraeus Archaeological Museum.

116 Athens. The sanctuary of Asklepios on the south slope of the Acropolis. It included the temple with the altar, the two-storey Doric stoa-enkoimeterion (dormitory), in which the patients were cured, of the second half of the 4th or the begining of the 3rd century BC, a second stoa of Roman times and the Ionic stoa-katagogion of the later 5th century BC.

116

Dionysia, the Lenaia, Olympieia, Arrephoria, Chalkeia, Thesmophoria, Haloa, Brauronia, seem to have already been as important as they were in Classical times.

The official State festivals included, by case, a procession, music, drama [fig. 113] or athletic contests and a torch race (*lampadedromia*). The climax of the celebrations was the sacrifice, frequently *en masse*, depending on the festival's significance, which was followed, circumstantially, by the consumption of the meat by the devotees. Some festivals also included a nocturnal vigil (*pannychis*) in the sanctuary, as for example the festivals of Demeter or the Panathenaia. In many festivals the official cultic ceremonial was accompanied by feasting and merrymaking, which in the festivals for Dionysos was heightened by an abundant consumption of wine.

Immediately after the battle of Marathon (490 BC) the Athenians wished to honour the goddess Athena for saving the land from the Persian threat. So they began to build on the Acropolis a propylon at the entrance to the sanctuary and, in about the same position as the Periclean Parthenon, a large temple of Pentelic marble, the first time this material was used in architecture. This temple is known to scholarship as the *Vorparthenon* or the Older Parthenon. However, when the temple was at the height of the second or third drum of the columns, the Acropolis, and the *Asty* too, was destroyed by the Persians and the temple burnt down. It seems that in this same period the first temple of Poseidon was erected at Sounion, while some scholars also consider as contemporary the small poros temple found under the foundations of the Classical temple of Athena Nike on the Acropolis.

After the Greeks' resounding victory over the Persians, and despite the oath they are said to have sworn before the battle of Plataiai (479 BC), to keep the ruins of the sanctuaries as permanent reminders of the barbarians' impiety, many devastated sanctuaries were rebuilt on the initiative of local *demoi* or individuals, while a few were included in a State building programme.

On the Acropolis, the destroyed architectural members and *ex-votos* were buried, while pieces of the Older Parthenon and the *Archaios Neos* were built into the north fortification wall of the Sacred Rock [figs 90, 121], possibly as a reminder of the catastrophe. Efforts to reconstitute the city were made in the

117

117 Athens, Acropolis. The north porch of the Erechteion.

time of Kimon, associated with whom is the building of the Doric temple of Hephaistos and Athena Ergane, as patron deities of metalworkers and craftsmen respectively, which began in 450/49 BC. Popularly known as the Theseion, this temple stands on the hill of Agoraios Kolonos [figs 58, 76, 132]. It is classed, on the basis of common features, in the same group as the temples of Poseidon at Sounion [figs 112, 144] and Nemesis at Rhamnous [figs 109, 110], as well as the temple that was relocated to the Agora in the reign of Roman emperor Augustus. This last one used to be identified as the temple of Ares at Acharnai [fig. 132], but it has been demonstrated recently that it was dedicated to Athena Pallenis. Also ascribed to the building activity under Kimon is the Doric temple of Apollo Delphinios and Artemis Delphinia, in the area of the Ilissos. In addition to these works, Kimon attended to the repair of the sanctuary of Eleusis.

However, the major building project of the Athenian State was organized in the time of Pericles and was implemented in the second half of the fifth cen-

118 Athens, Acropolis. The north side of the Parthenon, after the restoration works.

An intensive restoration programme of the Acropolis monuments commenced in 1975. Work on the Parthenon began in 1985 and is still in progress, aiming at the correction of previous interventions and the aesthetic restoration of the temple.

118

119 Athens. A relief marble plaque, possibly from the sanctuary of Aphrodite and Eros on the north slope of the Acropolis, with representation of a procession of Erotes moving left. They hold vases and vessels used in sacrifices (incense-burners, bowls-phialai and oinochoai-jugs). Second half of the 2nd century BC. Athens, National Archaeological Museum.

120 Athens. Plan with the monuments on the Acropolis hill.

1. Propylaia
2. Pinakotheke
3. Parthenon, temple of Athena Parthenos
4. Erechteion
5. Archaios Neos, temple of Athena Polias
6. Altar of Athena
7. Sanctuary of Zeus Polieus
8. Sanctuary of Pandion
9. House of Arrephoroi (Arrephoreion)
10. Temple of Rome and Augustus
11. Chalkotheke
12. Sanctuary of Artemis Brauronia
13. Temple of Athena Nike
14. Sanctuary of Apollo Hypoakraios
15. Sanctuary of Zeus Olympios
16. Sanctuary of Pan
17. Sanctuary of Aphrodite and Eros
18. Sanctuary of Aglauros
19. Sanctuary of Dionysos Eleuthereus
20. Sanctuary of Dionysos
21. Sanctuary of Asklepius
22. Temples of Thetis and Isis
23. Temples of Aphrodite Pandekos, Ge Kourotrophos and Demeter Chloe
24. Stoa of Eumenes B
25. Odeion of Herodes Atticus

tury BC. Its core was the religious centre of the city, the Acropolis, upon which were erected three Pentelic marble temples and the Propylaia [figs 65, 73, 90]. Works commenced with the building of the Parthenon (447–432 BC), which was consecrated in 438 BC, and the Propylaia (437–432 BC).

Tradition has it that the Parthenon [figs 73, 90, 118, 120, 121] which was initially called *Hekatompedos* (= one hundred feet) or *Megas Neos* (great temple) the name Parthenon was established for the temple as a whole in the fourth century BC, was built by the architects Kallikrates and Iktinos, while the general supervision and responsibility for the sculpted decoration and the chryselephantine cult statue of the goddess, was entrusted to the sculptor Pheidias [figs 70-72, 83, 86, 105–107]. The edifice was extended further north than the *Vorparthenon*, while its width was greater than the norm. In the Doric order, with Ionic elements, it had a pteron with 8x17 columns and an amphiprostyle hexastyle cella, around which ran a frieze. At the rear of the cella were four Ionic columns, while in the central part a two-tier, Π-shaped colonnade surrounded the statue of Athena [fig. 106]. The north pteron included a pre-existing simple cella, dedicated most probably to Athena Ergane or Pallas. Characteristic are the so-called visual refinements of the temple, such as the curvatures of the horizontal parts, the convergences of the vertical elements and the *entasis* (swelling) of the columns. The uniqueness of this monument lies in the excellence of the conception and execution of the design, in its harmonious proportions and the superb quality of the workmanship of the building and the sculptural decoration.

The Propylaia, in the Doric order, were designed by Mnesikles but remained unfinished, probably due to the outbreak of the Peloponnesian War [figs 90, 120, 121]. Apart from the central wing, which was the monumental entrance to the sanctuary, it included the south and the north wing, which housed the so-called Pinakotheke (= Picture Gallery), a place where pilgrims could rest and relax [fig. 67].

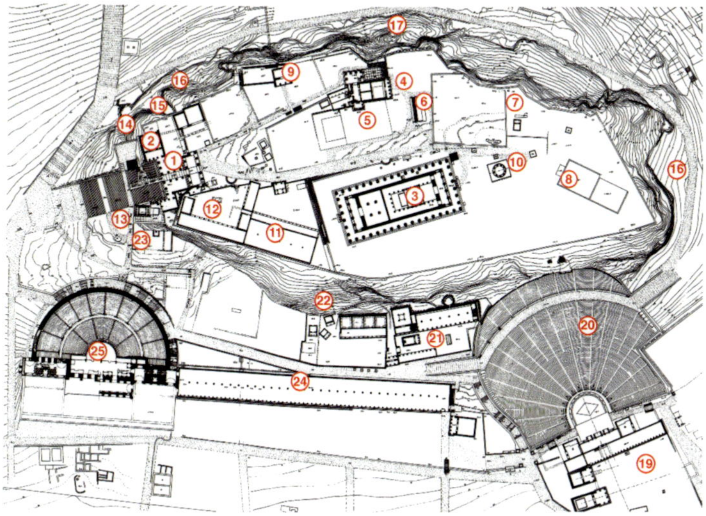

120

121 Athens. Reconstruction of The Acropolis hill from the north-west. Hellenistic period (late 4th–late 2nd century BC. (drawing by M. Korres).

121

122 Athens. View of the area of Ilissos by Johann Michael Wittmer. Partial detailed scene with the Temple of Olympian Zeus in the centre and the Acropolis to the left, watercolour (24 x 34.5 cm), Athens, 1833. In the foreground, a horseman is crossing the River Ilissos.

123 Athens. Engraving of the church of the Virgin at Petra, which had been built on the ruins of what is thought to be the Temple of Artemis Argotera, embodying the ancient material. The temple was destroyed and its remains were used for the construction of the wall by Turkish Voivode Hadji Ali Haseki, in 1778. The engraving, by J. Stuart and N. Revett (1751–1753), is of special significance, as it salvages elements of the ancient temple. Recent excavations have also revealed a second temple in the area.

The Erechtheion (421–413 BC and 409–406/5 BC) was built with interruptions, due to the war [fig. 117]. This name is encountered in later times, whereas in Antiquity it was known as the *"temple in the city, in which is the ancient statue'* or *"ancient temple"* or *"ancient temple of Athena Polias"*. In the Ionic order, the temple replaced the *Archaios Neos* [figs 69, 90, 120, 121] that was destroyed by the Persians, but its site was shifted a little northwards, perhaps in order to create a large free space between it and the altar, to facilitate the celebration of rites on the occasion of the Panathenaia festival. The attempt to create one other predecessor of it, probably in Early Classical times, has been ascertained. The temple housed the sacred signs and the worship of the most important deities and heroes referred to in the city's lore (Athena Polias, Poseidon Erechtheus, Boutes, Hephaistos, Kekrops, Zeus Hypatos), a fact that dictated its peculiar plan.

The elegant Ionic temple of Athena Nike [figs 88, 120, 121] was erected on the site of the pre-existing sanctuary and succeeded an earlier poros temple of debatable date, perhaps from the time of Kimon. Kallikrates was commissioned with its design and building of it was planned in the middle years of the century but did not take place until the late 430s–420s BC.

122

123

The subjects of the sculpted decoration of the aforesaid temples concerned the autochthony and the heroic struggles of the Athenians.

The Sacred Rock of the Acropolis [fig. 67] also hosted the sanctuaries of Zeus Polieus, Pandrosos, Artemis Brauronia, Pandion, Athena Hygeia, Hermes Propylaios, Hekate Epipyrgidia and the Graces. Ancillary buildings were the Arrephoreion, in which possibly resided the four little girls, the Arrephoroi, who served the goddess Athena annually, and the northwest building (priests' house, hestiatorion?).

There were several sanctuaries on the slopes of the Acropolis. The caves on the north slope [fig. 90] housed the cults of Apollo Hypoakraios, Zeus Olympios, Pan, Aphrodite and Eros [fig. 119], while on the east side was the sanctuary of Aglauros [figs 120, 121]. On the south slope there are indications of the formation of a second phase of the Theatre of Dionysos [fig. 114], while the Odeion of Pericles was also built there (447–442 BC) as a venue for music contests. Below the tower of Athena Nike were the sanctuaries of Aphrodite Pandemos and Peitho, as well as of Demeter Chloe and Ge Kourotrophos [fig. 67].

In the area of the Ilissos river [fig. 122], an Ionic temple was built in the third quarter of the fifth century BC. This has many features in common with the temple of Athena Nike and has been identified as the temple of Artemis Agrotera [fig. 123].

From around 460 to 420 BC, temples that vied in their art with those of Athens, were built in the Attic *chora*. These include at Sounion the temple of Athena and shortly after that of Poseidon [fig. 112], at Rhamnous the temple of Nemesis [fig. 110], at Pallene of Athena, while at Eleusis the new Telesterion was constructed in the time of Pericles [fig. 128]. Moreover, associated with the development of the port of the Piraeus after the Persian Wars are the sanctuaries of Zeus Soter and Athena Soteira, as well as that of Aphrodite at the Eetioneia Gate [fig. 176].

124 During the 4th century BC the sanctuary of Aphrodite at Daphni also enjoyed great popularity. From here come the two marble figurines of doves, the sacred bird of the goddess. On one is a dedicatory inscription to Aphrodite. Athens, National Archaeological Museum.

125 Daphni. View of the sanctuary of Aphrodite, on the road to Eleusis. In the rock-cut niches devotees placed votive offerings.

During the fifth century BC several changes occurred in traditional worship in Attica. Old cults were upgraded because of the happy outcome of the Persian Wars and the contribution that certain gods and heroes were believed to have made to this. These included Athena Nike at the west edge of the rock of the Acropolis, Herakles at Marathon, Artemis Agrotera on the banks of the Ilissos. So, some festivals acquired greater importance in the life of the worshippers, such as the Herakleia, the festival of Artemis "in the Fields" (Agrotera), where 500 she-goats were sacrificed to celebrate the victory at Marathon, the Aianteia on Salamis, in honour of the local hero Ajax, the Mounichia, the old festival of Artemis Mounichia, who was linked with the Greek victory over the Persians in the naval battle of Salamis (480 BC).

Some sanctuaries were repaired, primarily on private initiative. Well-known is the contribution of Themistocles to the repair of the Telesterion in the sanctuary of the Great Gods at Phlya (in about the same area as present Chalandri), the mystery cult of which was controlled by the *genos* of the Lykomidai, of which he was a scion.

In other cases sanctuaries were founded of heroes and gods with new hypostases, as *ex-votos* for the victories over the Persians, such as the sanctuary of Boreas in the area of the Ilissos, the sanctuary of Artemis Aristoboule founded by Themistocles at Melite, and the sanctuary founded by the Athenians with the booty from the battle of Marathon, in honour of Eukleia, an epithet of Artemis in other places. Furthermore, the cult of Zeus Eleutherios was established in the Agora, where the homonymous stoa was built [fig. 132].

126

126–128 Eleusis. The sanctuary of Demeter and Kore (Persephone) at Eleusis was one of the most important in Antiquity, of panhellenic renown where the two chthonic goddesses were worshipped as protectresses of life after death, fertility of the earth and, in particular, the cultivation of cereal crops [fig. 108]. It was a mystery cult, with eschatological and soteriological ramifications, and its main manifestation was the festival of the Great Mysteries, during which devotees were initiated.

The Great Mysteries were shrouded by strict secrecy, lasted nine days and were celebrated in autumn, from the 15th day of the month Boedromion (about late September). On the eve of the festival, sacred objects were brought to the Eleusinion in Athens, where they remained for five days, during the preliminary stage of the festival. On the first day, candidates for initiation announced their participation (agyrmos). The second day was devoted to purifications in the sea (helasis) of the candidates for initiation and of the pigs, sacred animals of Demeter, which were to be sacrificed. On the third day (hiereia deuro) the official sacrifice was made on behalf of the State and the cities that had sent "first fruits" (aparchai). On the fourth day (Epidaureia or Asklepieia) any latecomers had the opportunity to submit as candidates, while the rest indulged in contemplation and preparation for the initiation. On the 19th day of Boedromion, the sacred objects returned to Eleusis, accompanied by a multitudinous procession that set off from the Pompeion in the Kerameikos [fig. 58]. It seems that on the next day sacrifices were made in the sanctuary and prospective initiates were offered the pelanos (a kind of bread), after having previously fasted and drunk the potion kykeon. That night the initiation took place, with the revealing of the "sacred" by the hierophant, under shining light. On the next two days the dromena, the deiknymena and the legomena were performed. The second night was probably that of the epopteia, the highest degree of initiation. On the eighth day (plemochoe/ai) libations were made to the dead. The last day saw the departure of the faithful.

There were three stages in the initiation process. The first took place in winter, during the month of Anthesterion, on the occasion of the Minor Mysteries in the Metroon "in the Fields", at Athens. The second stage followed in the autumn, with initiation in the Great Mysteries at Eleusis, while the third, known as epopteia, was experienced one year later, at the same festival.

The red-figure pinax [fig. 126], which was dedicated by Ninnion in the sanctuary of Eleusis, *ca* 370 BC, is considered to illustrate moments from the Mysteries at Eleusis. Depicted are Demeter, Kore, perhaps also Iakchos and initiates. Some scholars doubt this interpretation. Athens, National Archaeological Museum.

The earliest remains of a cult building in the sanctuary were uncovered beneath the later Telesteria and are dated to Geometric times (8th c. BC). The excavators of the site considered that a megaron-type building with precinct of the Mycaenean times was the first temple of the goddess, although this view has not been widely accepted. The most important building in the sanctuary was the Telesterion, the locus sanctus of Demeter. The earliest Telesterion was constructed in the time of Solon (early 6th c. BC). At its rear was the Adyton or Anaktoron or Megaron, a rectangular space of small dimensions in which the sacred paraphernalia were kept and to which only the hierophantes had access. This space was kept in the later Telesteria too. The growing fame of the sanctuary led to the building of a new Telesterion, of square plan, the so-called Peisistratian, in the second half of the sixth century BC. As in the preceding phases, the Telesterion was surrounded by the sacred court.

In the mid-5th century BC, Pericles commissioned Iktinos to design a new larger Telesterion, which was built eventually with changes to the original bold plan, by the architect Koroibos. This was an edifice in the Doric order, almost square, with 42 columns in the interior and a prostasis on the east side. In the 4th century BC, the Philoneios Stoa was added to the façade of the Telesterion. The building was kept without changes until AD 170, when the entire sanctuary was destroyed in a hostile incursion. It was rebuilt, however, by Emperor Marcus Aurelius. The Telesterion dominates in fig. 127.

In order to protect the sanctuary, already from the 6th century BC a strong fortified enceinte (peribolos) had been constructed, the so-called Peisistratian, while due to the successive expansions of the sanctuary new enceintes were built in the 5th century BC (Periclean) and the 4th century BC (the so-called Lykourgan, although it began to be raised in 370/60 BC).

The sanctuary included also a built well, which has been identified as the Kallichoron (= of the Fair Dances) mentioned in the sources, where Demeter was believed to have taken rest on her arrival in Eleusis. A little temple in front of a cave, which was considered a point of communication between the upper and the under world, was dedicated to Pluto.

The multitudes of pilgrims and the reputation of the sanctuary created the need for infrastructure facilities. Concurrently, there was a host of diverse ex-votos. The entrance to the sanctuary, initially a simple gateway, was replaced by luxurious constructions in Roman times, the Lesser and the Great Propylaia [fig. 128], of the 1st and the 2nd century AD respectively. There were also various ancillary buildings, to serve the needs of devotees.

During the period of Roman rule, three new temples were built, the first dedicated to Poseidon Pater and Artemis Propylaia, and the other two to imperial cult. It is noteworthy that the sculptural decoration of the pediment of one of these temples copied the west pediment of the Parthenon.

South of the sanctuary stood the "Hiera Oikia" (sacred house), of the 8th century BC, in which traces of cult have been ascertained. It was replaced by a small temple in the 6th century BC, and a sanctuary of the god of eastern provenance, Mithras, was built in Roman times.

127

128

129 Athens, Pnyx. To the left of the speakers' platform there are salvaged niches that had been cut into the bedrock. These were of various sizes and in them were placed votive plaques dedicated to Zeus Hypsistos. The largest niche most probably contained the cult statue. In the past it was believed that worship had taken place in the area from the classical times. Recent view dates the sanctuary to the end of the 1st century AD.

130 Oropos. Marble relief, 400-350 BC. It was dedicated to Amphiaraos by Archinos. The relief depicts two consecutive phases in the curing of a patient. At the left by a god and at the right, during his sleep, by a snake. Athens, National Archaeological Museum.

Finally, the worship of Pan was introduced from Arkadia, since this god was also accredited with the victorious outcome of the battle of Marathon. Sanctuaries dedicated to him were founded in Athens, such as in the cave on the north slope of the Acropolis [fig. 90] or on the Pnyx [fig. 129]. His cult combined with that of the Nymphs was accommodated in caves in the rural territory of Attica, as at Vari, Oinoe near Marathon, on Pentele, Hymettos and Parnes, at Daphni [figs 124, 125] and Eleusis.

The outcome of the consequences of the plague that struck Athens during the Peloponnesian War was the introduction to Attica of the worship of the *par excellence* healing god, Asklepios, first to the Piraeus [fig. 115] and perhaps one year later, in 420/19 BC, to Athens, by Telemachos from Acharnai, who founded the sanctuary on the south slope of the Acropolis [fig. 116]. The tragic poet Sophocles received the god "by shaking hands" (*dexiosis*) and was venerated posthumously with the epithet Dexion. These examples reveal the particular promotion of the individual in this period, even in one of the most conservative sectors of Athenian life, religion. Apollo, Athena, Artemis, Aphrodite, Herakles, Amynos, Amphiaraos (at Oropos and Rhamnous), Aristomachos (at Rhamnous) were also worshipped as deities with healing powers, as were the "*heroes physicians*" (at Athens, Eleusis and Marathon).

A special case is the worship of Kybele, a goddess of Phrygian provenance, identical to the Mother of the Gods, which was organized in particular during the fifth century BC. There were cult places on the west side of the Agora, in the Pnyx, in the area of the Ilissos, where the Lesser Mysteries in the Fields were celebrated, in the Piraeus and Moschato. Worship of the god Sabazios, also of Phrygian origin, was related to that of Kybele.

129

The settling of foreigners, mainly merchants, in Attica led to the gradual introduction of their local cults, with permission from the Athenian State. Thus, in 429 BC a sanctuary of the Thracian deity Bendis was founded in the Piraeus, mainly for political reasons. Her festival, which included a sacrifice, two processions, an all-night vigil (*pannychis*) and a torch-race (*lampadedromia*) on horseback, attracted a big crowd of devotees.

With the fall of Athenian hegemony the city's major festivals, the Panathenaia and the Great Dionysia, lost much of their splendour, since the allies who heretofore took part in these, either voluntarily or compulsorily, with one ox and one panoply, ceased to contribute.

The introduction of new cults is observed in the fourth century BC. In 333 BC, merchants from Kition on Cyprus founded a sanctuary of Aphrodite Ourania and Adonis. The cult of Aphrodite Ourania was possibly already practised on the north side of the Agora, while a "money-box" (*thesauros*) of the early fourth century BC, found on the Acropolis, was intended to collect drachmas as "advance payment for marriage" (*proteleia gamou*) in her honour. Although worship of the Egyptian goddess Isis was introduced in this period, it was not espoused officially by the Athenians until much later. A sanctuary and a festival existed of one other Egyptian deity, Ammon. The 4th century was generaly an era of flourishing of many sanctuaries [figs 130, 131].

Another characteristic of Athenian religion in the fourth century BC was the emphasis on the cult of personified concepts, which allude to political life, such as Demokratia (Democracy), Eirene (Peace) and Agathe Tyche (Good Fortune).

In the early fourth century BC, two buildings were constructed to serve the needs of the sanctuaries and of cult. One was the Chalkotheke on the Acropolis (probably 394/3–390 BC), in which the metal *ex-votos* of the sanctuary were kept, and the other was the Pompeion in the Kerameikos (*ca* 400 BC) [fig. 58], which was not only a gymnasium but also a place for safekeeping the sacred paraphernalia of the Panathenaic procession, as well as for organizing the procession and the banquets for the officials participating in the festival.

In the second half of the fourth century BC, the Lykourgos, an astute politician and member of the *genos* that provided the priestesses of Athena Polias and the priests of Poseidon Erechtheus, was the first to draft a religious policy, with the aim of reorganizing worship and the sanctuaries. His inspired economic policy secured sufficient wealth to reform the sacred places and to promote traditional cults. In this task he was also helped by the input of private citizens.

Lykourgos' building programme made provision for repairs or additions to existing temples and to the completion of unfinished edifices. His archonship saw the construction of the new bigger stone theatre, the stoa and peribolos in the sanctuary of Dionysos Eleuthereus [fig. 114], which had been preceded by the construction of the new temple to the god. For the needs of events associated with the Panathenaia and the Great Dionysia festivals [fig. 113], the Stadium was constructed in the Ardettos valley [fig. 45]. According to a recent view, an attempt was made to complete the temple of Zeus Olympios in the same area. In the Agora, the two temples of Apollo Patroos, father of Ion, leading ancestor of the Athenians, and of Zeus Phratrios and Athena Phratria, were built, while the temple of Artemis

130

131 Oropos. The Sanctuary of Amphiaraus underwent a great development after the Battle of Chaeronea (338 BC), when the town of Oropos came under Athenian rule, and up until the 1st century BC. Amphiaraus, one of the Seven Against Thebes, was worshipped at Oropos as a chthonic deity with therapeutic and psychic powers from the end of the 5th century BC. During antiquity it was a health care centre. The temple was built in the 4th century BC and possessed a pronaos and an alcove with three aisles, while the small space at the back of the alcove was considered an adyton, due to the chthonic status of the deity. The sanctuary also included a font, a theatre, a 110m stoa which was the *enkoimeterion* (dormitory) of the faithful, a market with a row of statues on its facade, public baths, a hydraulic clock (*clepsydra*) and areas for accommodating visitors.

131

132 The Athenian Agora, 150 AD (drawing by W.B. Dinsmoor Jr).

1. Panathenaic way
2. Altar of the Twelve Gods
3. Stoa of Zeus
4. Temple of Apollo Patroos
5. Hephaesteion
6. Tholos
7. Bouleuterion
8. Metroon
9. Eponymous heroes
10. Boundary stones
11. Prison
12. Southwest fountain house
13. Aiakeion
14. South stoa I
15. Southeast fountain house
16. Mint
17. Middle stoa
18. East building
19. South stoa II
20. Late roman fortification
21. Library of Pantainos
22. Stoa of Attalos
23. Lawcourrs
24. Odeion of Agrippa
25. Temple of Ares / Athena Pallenis
26. Crossroads shrine
27. Royal stoa
28. Stoa Poikile
29. Southwest temple
30. Houses
31. Nymphaion
32. Eleusinion
33. Library of Hadrian
34. Roman agora
35. Monopteros
36. Roman basilica
37. Altar of Aphrodite Ourania

Aristoboule was repaired at the expenses of Neoptolemos from Melite. At Eleusis a stoa designed by the Eleusinian architect Philon was added to the façade of the Telesterion, and was completed towards the end of the century [fig. 127]. Works in the sanctuary of Dionysos in the *demos* of Ikaria (pres. Dionysos) were also associated with Lykourgos' reorganization.

New music and drama contests were added to the programme of festivals, and equestrian games to the Eleusinia. With the regaining of Oropos in 336 BC, Lykourgos showed particular interest in the sanctuary of Amphiaraos. A new temple was built and the quinquennial games were included in the Attic festive calendar [fig. 131]. The reorganization of the institution of *Ephebeia* in the time of Lykourgos was based *inter alia* on respect for the gods of the traditional cult, while it was predicated on the more active participation of the ephebes in the festivals, many of which were enriched with sacrifices, processions and contests with ships of young Athenians.

In Hellenistic times there appeared in Attica, as in the rest of Greece, the phenomenon of ruler worship. It began with the liberator of Athens in 307 BC, Demetrios Poliorketes, and his father Antigonos Monophthalmos, who were worshipped as Saviours (*Soteres*) and in whose honour the Demetria festival was instituted. Concurrently, the rulers of the various kingdoms vied with one another in showing their respect for the patron goddess of the city, Athena.

The major Attic festivals continued in existence until Roman times and were celebrated most splendidly, very often thanks to the generosity of individuals. However, rural cults seem to have weakened to such a degree, with the downgrading of the *demoi* as organizers of religious life, that in the reign of Augustus temples housing important cults in the *demoi* were transferred to the Agora of Athens [fig. 132]. Other cults seem to have lost the interest of devotees, while the development of the philosophical schools in Athens had a constraining effect on the observance of traditional cult. The devastation of the Attic countryside by Philip V in 200 BC also played a part in the desertion of the sanctuaries.

The influence of affluent citizens on worship in this period is apparent even in the holding of sacerdotal offices. Indicative too is the founding of the cult of the Demos and the Graces (Charites), towards the end of the third century BC, on the initiative of two brothers, Eurykleides and Mikion, political figures of the time, or even the worship of eminent citizens as heroes.

The addition of new celebrations and games or sacrifices to existing festivals, in commemoration of historical events or persons, continued also in Hellenistic times, as for example the Diogenia festival which was founded in honour of Diogenes, to whom was owed the liberation of Attica in 229 BC, or the Ptolemaia, which were established shortly before the death of Ptolemy III, in 221 BC.

Yet another characteristic of the period is the spread of worship of gods or heroes with therapeutic and soteriological qualities, as well as of foreign deities, such as Serapis, mainly by various religious associations of non-Athenian citizens. The plethora of cults in the period is also attested by the inscriptions on the thrones in the Theatre of Dionysos [fig. 54], which designated the seats of the priests or priestesses of the diverse deities worshipped by the Athenians [fig. 133].

The evolution of worship in Roman times was similar. Some sanctuaries were abandoned, new ones were founded (temples housing imperial cult or the temple of Tyche/Fortuna on Ardettos hill, founded by Herodes Atticus, and perhaps the sanctuary of Zeus Hypsistos at Pnyx), while others extant or destroyed in 86 BC by Sulla, were rebuilt, mainly on the initiative of Roman emperors or other kings.

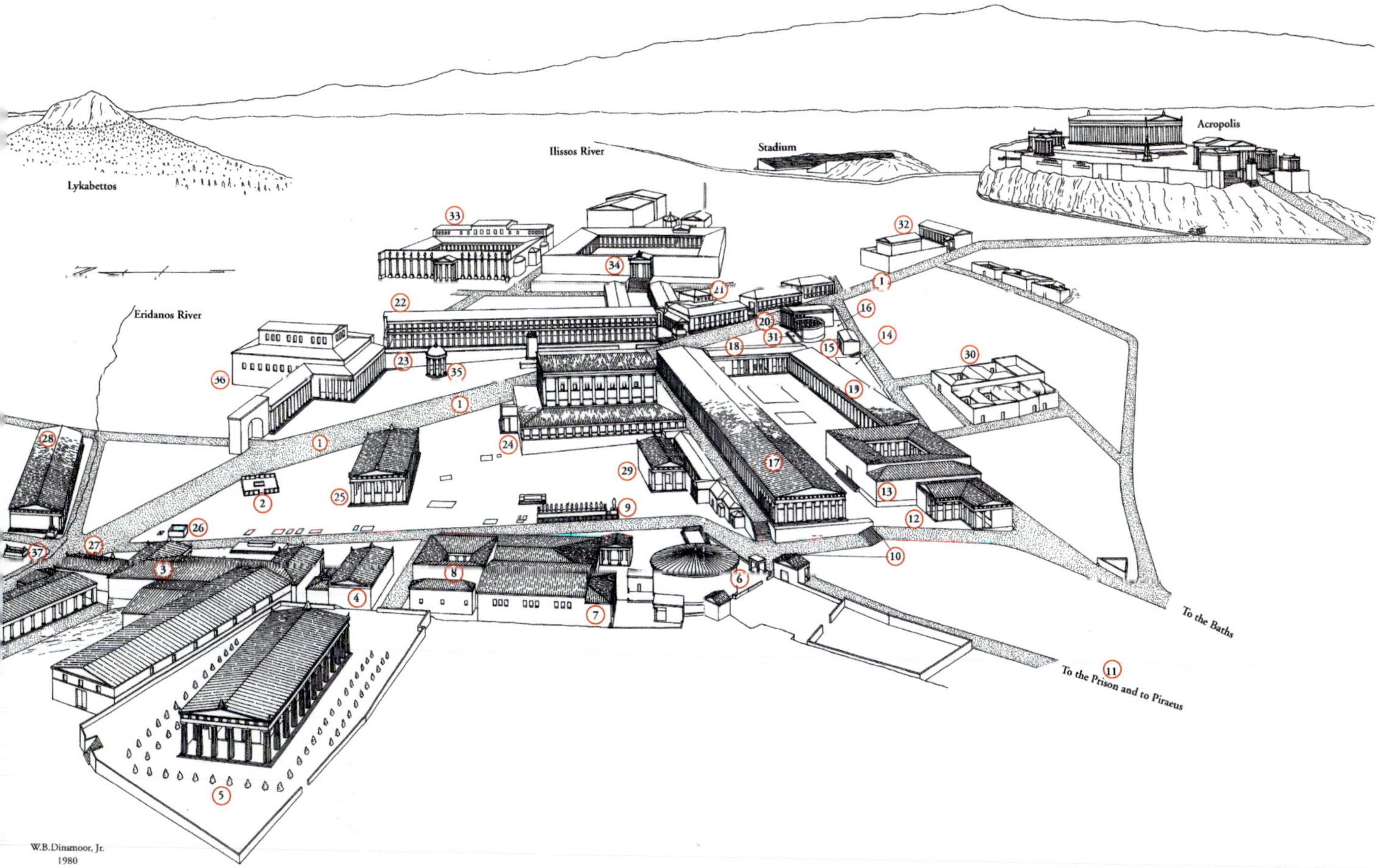

On the Acropolis, a small monopteral temple was erected in honour of Roma and Augustus [fig. 53], extensive repairs were made to the Erechtheion and, in the reign of Claudius (AD 51/2), the ramp giving access to the Sacred Rock was converted into a staircase.

In the Agora, in the late first century BC, temples for imperial cult were built of *spolia* from older temples in the Attic *chora*, and one entire temple of the fifth century BC, dedicated to Athena Pallenis, was relocated there. Also, parts of the temple of Athena Sounias and the unfinished temple(?) at Thorikos, which some scholars have identified as a temple of Demeter, were used in building these temples. Two spaces at the rear of the Stoa of Zeus Eleutherios were dedicated to imperial cult, while the altar of Zeus Agoraios was transferred from the Pnyx.

Outside the *Asty*, in AD 45/6 the temple of Nemesis at Rhamnous was dedicated to the deified Livia, wife of Augustus, while in the sanctuary of Eleusis two temples dedicated to imperial cult were erected in a conspicuous position.

Several decades later, in the second century AD, Emperor Hadrian [fig. 80] demonstrated especial interest in the city of Athens and particularly in the area of the Ilissos. It was in his reign that, after centuries of effort, the temple of Zeus Olympios was finally completed [figs 56, 90], in the Corinthian order, and was consecrated during the emperor's visit to Athens, in AD 131/2. In the same period the Panhellenion was built, where the Panhellenion *Koinon* met and Zeus Panhellenios and Hera were worshipped, as well as Hadrian, also as Panhellenios. In all probability, in the framework of the general programme of remodelling the area, the temple of Kronos and Rhea was built too, in the mid-second century AD. One other building for cult purposes erected in Hadrian's reign was the Pantheon, in which all the gods were worshipped (building in Adrianou Street). The emperor was also benefactor of the sanctuary of Demeter at Eleusis [figs 126–128], where he himself was initiated into the Mysteries in AD 125.

A few years later, the wealthy benefactor Herodes Atticus [fig. 79] reconstructed the Stadium of Pentelic marble (AD 139/40–143/4), which could accommodate 50,000 spectators. On Ardettos hill he built a temple of Tyche/Fortuna, first priestess of which was his wife Regilla. Finally, on the south slope

133

133 Athens, Ancient Agora. Ivory statuette of Apollo, which reproduces the statue type of Apollo Lykeios. 2nd or 3rd century AD. The original, a creation probably of 340–330 BC, which has been associated with Praxiteles, stood in the sanctuary of Apollo Lykeios. Cult of the god was linked with the Lykeion Gymnasium (Lyceum), one of the gymnasia of Athens, located in the east of the city, north of the River Ilissos, where young men exercised and were educated. Athens, Museum of the Ancient Agora.

134

134 Marathon. Large clay lamp with busts of Serapis and Isis from the sanctuary of the Egyptian gods. It is assumed that they illuminated the nocturnal rituals in honour of Isis. Marathon Archaeological Museum.

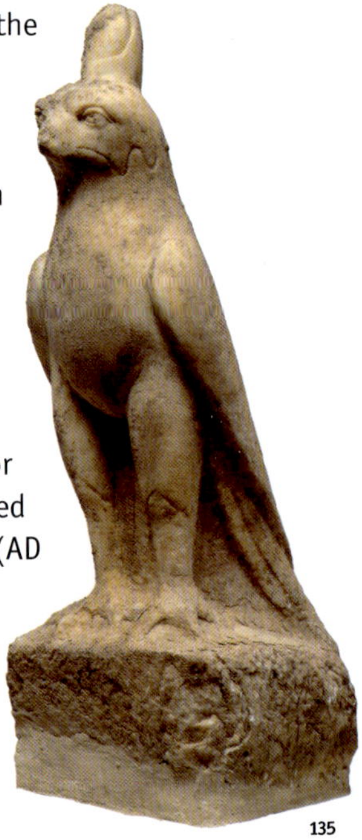
135

of the Acropolis he built a new Odeum [figs 73, 120], after Regilla's death in AD 161. Herodes was also interested in sanctuaries in other areas, such as of Nemesis at Rhamnous or of Athena at Myrrhinous, but above all in the sanctuaries of his place of origin, Marathon. Linked with his name is the luxurious sanctuary of the Egyptian gods at Brexiza [figs 134–137], where offerings from him have been found, and a building at Oinoe, which is considered to be part of the sanctuary of Apollo Pythios.

It appears that worship of the ancient gods was kept alive in Attica until the fourth century AD, as the archaeological evidence attests. It was finally abolished with the edicts issued by Emperor Theodosius I the Great. The most revered sanctuaries of Attica, renowned throughout the ancient world, were deserted or were converted into Early Christian basilicas, in order to house the worship of the new religion, Christianity.

136

137

135 Marathon. Statue of Horus as a falcon wearing the crown of Upper Egypt, from the sanctuary of the Egyptian gods. Marathon Archaeological Museum.

136 Marathon. Statue of Antinoos-Osiris from the western porch of the sanctuary of the Egyptian gods. Antinoos was Hadrian's young favourite. 2nd century AD. Marathon Archaeological Museum.

137 Marathon. The sanctuary of the Egyptian gods, located in the marsh at Brexiza, beside the sea, was founded in the 2nd century AD. Preserved is part of the square enclosure (peribolos) of the sanctuary, with a monumental propylon in the middle of each side. The entrances were flanked internally and externally by two statues in Egyptian style, male and female, of which two male and one female have been found (exhibited in the Marathon Museum and in the Egyptian Collection of the National Archaeological Museum, Athens). Paved processional causeways led from the entrances to the square temple, which was surrounded by various rooms.

Attic *demoi*

GEORGE STEINHAUER

The geography of the Attica Peninsula, its mythology and the ruins of the Mycenaean palace on the rock of the Acropolis (shortly before 1200 BC) leave no doubt that Attica (the Athens basin, the interior plain of the Mesogeia and the coastal plains of Marathon and perhaps of Eleusis) had been a single kingdom in Mycenaean times.

It is very possible that the Middle Helladic (2000–1600 BC) and Late Helladic (1600–1100 BC) forts at Aphidnai, Mounichia, Brauron, Thorikos, Lamptrai, the "royal" tholos tombs at Acharnai and Marathon, the centres with the wealthy cemeteries at Spata, Pallini, Glyfada and Vari — preserved in memory by the list of the twelve cities of Kekrops —, and the sites of the original settlement of the major Attic clans, provided the ancient nucleus of many of the later *demoi*.

Some idea of the settlement pattern in Athens and Attica in the so-called Geometric period (9th–8th centuries BC) is given by the scant remains of scattered houses, workshops and roads in the Athens basin, and the complex at Lathoureza near Vari, as well as the dispersion of the Geometric cemeteries (north: Nea Ionia, Kifissia and Marathon; west: Kokkinia, Trachones, Vari and Anavyssos; in the Mesogeia: Merenda and Markopoulo), which gradually covered the whole of Attica. The progress of the synoecism of Athens, which possibly played a leading role in the basin and in the various provincial *tetrakomiai* (of Marathon, of Pallene, of the Mesogaia, of the Piraeus), but not in Eleusis, is illustrated by the long history of the cemetery and the high art (as well as the thematic repertoire) of the Dipylon vases in the Kerameikos [fig. 59]. Within this framework, the role of the great aristocratic clans [fig. 139] which, from the urban centre or in their seats in the rural towns, controlled the political life, agricultural production and (trading) relations with the *Asty* and abroad, as well as the dangers this harboured for the unity and concord of Attica, was to acquire specific form in the successive crises during the seventh and sixth centuries BC, which Drakon, Solon and Peisistratos were called upon to handle, thus preparing the way for the unification of Attica. Their groundwork was completed by Kleisthenes, with the administrative synoecism of the entire population of Attica, an enor-

138

138 Kallithea. Black-figure lekythos with representation of the sacrifice of a he-goat in front of a herm. Early 5th century BC, from a grave at Kallithea. Piraeus Archaeological Museum.

139

139 Attica. In the grave statue of the aristocratic youth Aristodikos, the tendency to free the figure of the Archaic kouros scheme is apparent, while the inner strength and self-awareness of the Athenian at the dawn of the new age of the Persian Wars and of Tragedy are recognized. *Ca* 500 BC. From Olympos, south-west Attica. Athens, National Archaeological Museum.

mous area (2,500 sq. m.) by Greek standards, in the city-state of the Athenians. Through the single organization of the population in new tribes, *trittyes* and *demoi*, which bridged the geographical and social gap that had always divided the city-dweller, noble, artisan or merchant, from the farmer in the countryside, he set the bases for the isonomy (legal and political equality) and concord between *asty* and *chora*, upon which, in contrast to the centralizing model of Sparta, the Athenian democracy was founded.

The cornerstone of Kleisthenes' reform was the *demos*. The initial number of *demoi* is not known. In the fourth century BC, 139 *demoi* are attested epigraphically, which, depending on their geographical location, in the environs of the *Asty*, in the littoral zone or in the hinterland, were distributed in corresponding local (urban, coastal and mountainous) subdivisions (*trittyes*) of the ten new tribes, which could have from one very large *demos* (such as Acharnai) to eight small ones [fig. 140].

Politically the *demos* was at once a self-governing portion of the Attic population, a specific geographical area of Attica and a decentralized nuclear unit of the Athenian State: the registry office, the army recruitment bureau, the electoral centre and, in a way, the mortgage office of Athens. The citizen body assembled and decided, just like the *ekklesia* of the *demos* of the Athenians, on all local issues, principally economic and religious, such as the leasing of demotic landholdings, the organization of festivals [fig. 141], the conferring of honours on archons and *choregoi*, and so on. It elected the local authorities, the *demarchos* and the representatives of the *demos* in the *boule* the treasurers (*tamiai*), the temple magistrates (*hieropoioi*), and so on. The *demarchos* convened and chaired the assembly, carried out its decisions and was the link with the State. Regardless of where an Athenian was domiciled, the *demos* was sentimentally his homeland, while practically it represented the collective memory and guaranteed the validity of his marriage, his children and the boundaries of his property. The strong tie between *demotai* and their home *demos*, even when they (no small number) no longer resided there, is attested by the gatherings in the demotic meeting places in Athens, their concern for community affairs, the family tomb enclosures encountered at the edge of fields, and the love for this place, which was confirmed each year at harvest time or the vintage, at festivals and fairs of the *demos*. The festivals were usually held in winter, in the months of Posideon and Gamelion (December-January) when the earth sleeps and there is a lull in farming tasks. The Dionysia *kat' agrous* ("at the fields") were one of the most pleasurable moments in the monotonous life of the little village, with the procession parodied by Aristophanes in *Acharnians*, the sacrifice and the contest in the little theatre of the *demos*, such as those known at Thorikos [figs 149, 150], Ikarion, Rhamnous [fig. 145], Euonymon, Alimos and as has been revealed recently Acharnai, or others

140 Map of Attica showing the sites of the ancient demoi. The size of the dot corresponds to that of the population, as estimated on the basis of the number of elected bouleutai.

known only from inscriptions. Relatives and childhood friends congregated here and renewed their ties, far from the travails of the law courts and of politics. Eating and drinking were accompanied by simple entertainments, songs, improvised games and contests, while all around were stalls with children's toys. At the festival of the phratries, the Apatouria, the clansmen gathered around the altar of Zeus Phratrios received the new members of their phratry, in a rite that was repeated at puberty and was a precondition for registering the child in the citizens' roll. An idea of the space is given by the sanctuary of Zeus Phratrios, with the simple room for the assemblies and the altar next to the well, which was excavated recently in the *demos* of Myrrhinous. The venues of the assemblies of the *orgeones*, *thiasoi*, *eranoi* should be imagined as more or less like this, where these frequently related religious associations gathered on the set day of their tutelary god or hero, in order to honour him with sacrifice [fig. 138] and a hearty communal repast in his sanctuary, in the middle of the fields. Only the extremely strong emotive tie that linked the Athenians with their *demos* and life in the fields can explain the deep sorrow of the inhabitants of Attica at the forced abandonment of the countryside (Thucydides II.16) or the nostalgia of Dikaiopolis (Aristophanes, *Acharnians*, 28–36) who, isolated *intra muros* of the city, thinks of his village.

The connective tissue of this democratic state was the dense road network, which radiated out from Athens, linking with each other and with the centre the *demoi* of each *trittys*, and so facilitating the access of *demotai* to the *Asty*, in order to participate in the decision-making process, in meting out justice, in the major festivals and games [fig. 166], as well as in manning the Athenian army and navy. Recent excavations have revealed large parts of this network, which consists of straight dirt roads about 3.50 m wide, bordered by low walls, many of which, not surprisingly, follow exactly the same route as today's main road arteries [fig. 143] of Kifissias, Mesogeion, Marathonos and Spaton avenues.

141

141 Spata. The inscription entitled "Δημαρχία ή μείζων" contains a list of the festivals and sacrifices celebrated each month by the demos of Erchia, in the vicinity of Spata, where it was found. Athens, Epigraphical Museum.

If our knowledge of the form, function and political role of the Attic *demoi* is owed basically to Aristotle's *Athenian Constitution*, to the inscriptions, the advocates (Isaios, Lysias and primarily Demosthenes), the comic poets (Aristophanes, Menander), the historians and the later geographers and travellers (Strabo, Pausanias), our reconstruction of the settlement pattern of Attica and the form of the Attic *demos* is owed almost exclusively to archaeological research, particularly that of the last decades. Beginning from the area of the Athens basin, *extra muros* of the city and in a zone reaching southeast as far as Alimos, east as far as Hymettos, north as far as Kifissia, northwest as far as Parnitha (anc. Parnes) and Aigaleo, spreads a pleasant, cultivated landscape punctuated only by family tomb enclosures, giving it a grandeur unknown to us built on the roadside, with low walls,

142 Pallini. Ruins of a complex of three farmhouses, isolated in the middle of the fields, with the rooms of each house arranged around a central court. Excavated during the construction of the Attiki Odos, in the area of Pallini. Dated to the late 4th century BC.

143 Spata. Classical road running parallel to the present Loutsa road, at the northern limit of the airport at Spata. On the left edge of the aerial photograph, the road intersected with another one, which was the main north-south axis of the Mesogeia. Visible bottom right are traces of the earlier Archaic road and the Geometric cemetery.

142

143

140

144 Sounion. The rocky promontory of Sounion rises 80 m a.s.l., opposite the vast expanse of the Aegean. Rock and sea are united on high by the airy colonnade of the temple of Poseidon. The terrace and the rectangular enceinte of the sanctuary dominate the summit of the cape, above the fortified settlement that extended on the slopes (at the centre of the aerial photograph), where traces of the main street and of the walls of the buildings are faintly visible. On the left edge are preserved remnants of the ship-sheds (neosoikoi).

145 Rhamnous. The fortified demos of Rhamnous, built on a hill slope at the north end of Attica, controlled the safety of the sea passage from the Euboean Gulf for ships loaded with grain and destined for Athens. This is the most fully excavated and published demos in Attica. At the centre of the aerial photograph can be seen the gateway and the main thoroughfare, which separates the complex of the agora, the gymnasium and the theatre from the densely-built settlement on the right, as well as the fort with the military installations, on the hilltop. By contrast, no traces have survived of the now silted up double harbour at the foot of the hill.

145

146, 147 Rhamnous. The restored tomb enclosure of the brothers Athenodoros and Dromokles, sons of Atheneus. One of the most luxurious enclosures of the wealthy families of the demos, which lined the road from Athens and Marathon, that led through the sanctuary of Nemesis to the settlement of Rhamnous. Only three plain stelai were set up in the enclosure, along with one marble loutrophoros. Illustrated is the stele of Athenodoros, which is crowned by an elaborate palmette. The relief representation of a loutrophoros indicates that Athenodoros died unmarried. Rhamnous Archaeological Collection.

146

planted along their entire length with olive trees. The farmsteads [fig. 138], even in the relatively distant *demos* of Acharnai, were few and far between, since the inhabitants of the suburban *demoi* usually resided permanently in the city and journeyed to and fro, depending on their tasks in the fields, much like the unfortunate Eratosthenes in the oration of that name by Lysias.

It is characteristic of the way of life in the Attic countryside, as this has been revealed by excavations, that of the Attic *demoi* of the fourth century BC excepting those *intra muros* of Athens or the Hippodamean city of the Piraeus, very few seem to correspond to the settlement type of the modern Greek village.

Densely-built settlements are not encountered, except crammed inside the walls of the fortified *demoi* that are linked with the defence of Attica, the ancient city of Eleusis, the colony of Salamis, the forts of Rhamnous and Sounion, or where the needs of coordinated craft industrial production imposed it, as in the village of Thorikos. A typical example of a densely-built settlement is offered by Rhamnous, a site excellently excavated and published, which occupies the summit and the east slopes of a hill overlooking the sea, at the north end of the enclosed Limiko plain [fig. 145]. As the road from Marathon nears the village beyond the sanctuary of Nemesis [figs 109, 110], it is lined by the tomb enclosures of prominent families of the *demos* [figs 146, 147]. Two harbours at the foot of the hill served the nautical patrols in the Euboean Gulf, as well as fishermen and traders. The plan of the settlement is simple and the public buildings are plain. At the centre of the esplanade in front of the entrance to the acropolis is the agora, flanked by two public buildings and one stoa, which separates it from the gymnasium (or the lower camp, as it is called), while closing the third side is the theatre, identified by the alignment of the five thrones of the front row (*prohedria*). The entire east side of the hill is covered by a densely-built settlement, the neighbourhoods of which are separated by streets, most of them narrow and steep, and therefore unsuitable for wheeled vehicles, and small squares onto which open the front doors of the humble houses of irregular plan. The acropolis, where the garrison must have been stationed, presents a similar picture. Notable among the main bulk of the settlement, between the gateway and the agora, is an *insula* with two houses, one of them with a circular tower and the other with a courtyard flanked on two sides by rooms, including the *oikos* and the *andron* with five couches.

In contrast to Rhamnous, the likewise fortified settlement of Sounion (413/2 BC), located at the opposite southend of Attica, had been designed upon a rectangular ("Hippodamean") grid that covered the entire slightly sloping area (approx. 200x100 m) lying to the north of the sanctuary of Poseidon [fig. 144]. A central thoroughfare orientated east-west separates the spacious (250 sq. m.) urban residences with marble thresholds, corridors, internal courts and large cisterns, which were probably intended for members of the garrison. Again in contrast to Rhamnous, habitation here extended *extra muros*, along the west shore of the promontory, where traces of harbour installations and of one stoa have been identified. Farmhouses alternating with tomb enclosures, dozens of *ergasteria* (washeries for metal ore) and hundreds of mine galleries essentially cover the whole area of the *demos*, an enormous industrial park. Particularly dense is the concentration of tunnels and washeries [figs 51, 148] north of Sounion, in the continuous vales of Agrileza and Souriza, which were controlled by a network of towers, among which along the road of the *Asty* is a series of farmsteads, bearing witness to some agricultural activity in parallel with mining. Settlement units and tombs continue in sparser arrangement to the west, as far as the border with the *demos* of Amphitrope. Secondary settlement centres existed around the Pountazeza headland (5 km north of Sounion), east and west of which lie the sheltered bay of Panormos with the *Herakleion upon the Strait* (traces of a mole and a street leading inland, as well as a row of furnaces are still visible), and the neighbouring Pasha Limani, with a large (56x62 m) agora with workshops, which was subsequently the core of a Hellenistic settlement.

The picture of the neighbouring *demos* of Thorikos is analogous to that of the *demos* of Sounion intermediate between the fortress village of Rhamnous and the multi-nucleated settlement, which will be discussed below. The central settlement, which occupies the southwest slopes of Velatouri hill, over-

147

148 Souriza, Sounion. The "Asklepiakon" ergasterion of Simos from Paiania, one of the largest and best-preserved washeries for silver ore in the Souriza valley. In addition to the washery installations and the storehouses, the ergasterion had dormitories and a bathhouse for the labourers and one house with an andron for the owner.

149 Merenda. Bronze theatre "ticket" from the sanctuary of the north cemetery of the ancient demos of Myrrhinous. Brauron Archaeological Museum.

150 Thorikos. The theatre of the ancient demos is dated to the 5th century BC. The form of the cavea, which reproduces the wooden bleachers (ikria), adapted to the rectangular orchestra, is encountered in theatres of many demoi (Ikarion, Euonymon, Rhamnous). The well-built retaining wall is associated with the extension in the 4th century BC. Abutting it to east and west were respectively a large assembly hall and the temple of Dionysos.

148

looking the harbour and the little coastal plain with the double Doric stoa usually identified as the temple of Demeter, gives the impression as at Rhamnous of a maze of streets, courtyards and rooms (all stone-built on the bedrock), in which ground plans of specific houses are difficult to decipher. Here too, at the central crossroad, there is a building complex of the early fifth century BC, comprising two houses and one large circular tower. In a later phase the two houses were united, and in the fourth century BC the west edge of the *insula* was extended by the addition of two new houses of more regular plan, reminiscent of the arrangement of houses in Priene, Asia Minor. At the edge of the settlement adjacent to the metal-ore washeries and the entrance to a mine gallery is the ellipsoidal theatre of the *demos* (considered to be the earliest in Greece, fig. 150) and the temple of Dionysos. There is epigraphic reference to an agora. Lower down, at least four houses with tower, set in gardens and fields, were excavated, along with workshops, sanctuaries and cemeteries, while an arc of farmsteads surrounds the settlement at some distance from it.

In the fourth century BC, most of the *demoi* known from excavations, on the west coast (Euonymon, Alimous, Aixone, Halai Aixonides, Anargyrous, Lamptrai, Thorai), on the edges of the Athens and the Mesogaia basins (Pallene, Ionidai, Kydantidai, Myrrhinous) and Marathon, have a pattern of loose habitation, with two or three settlement nuclei, usually along the main roads or around their intersection, about 600 or 700 m apart. The houses, 90 to 200 sq. m. at most, with courtyard and partially two-storeyed, are little different from those of the *Asty*. Built at the edge of the field or the far end of the garden, they usually alternate with family tomb enclosures and with small sanctuaries [figs 153, 154, 158, 159, 163], which are mentioned frequently in inscriptions as boundaries of properties. Not uncommonly, isolated houses or complexes of two or three houses (see below), a threshing floor or an agricultural storehouse are encountered, rarer in the far reaches (*eschaties*), thus forming an outer, sparsely settled zone that reached to the outermost limits of the *demos*, the domain of Pan and the Nymphs [fig. 152]. Even so, distances were never so great as to ruin the most important element of demotic life, the sense of neighbourliness with all this entails, good and bad; the mutual assistance essential for carrying out farming tasks and the solidarity in the face of the danger of hostile attack, as well as, on the other side, the endless disputes over fences, drains and sewers. As can easily be understood from the map [fig. 140], the distance between the boundaries of the *demos*, which were traditionally defined by geographical features, a hill or stream (only at the end of the fourth century BC were some *demoi*, such as Lamptrai, Amphitrope, Sounion, etc., delimited with "*horoi*" (boundary markers) carved on the rock [fig. 151], did not exceed 3–4 km, that is no more than one hour's walk. This meant that the greatest distance a person had to cover from his house to the religious centre, the theatre or the agora of the *demos* was, even in the extreme case of the inhabitant of the far reaches, at most 20 to 30 minutes. The picture agrees with what is known about the population of the *demoi*. On the basis of the electoral measure, that is, the ratio of 42 *demotai* (men with the rights of citizen) to one *bouleutes* (deputy), the total number of families and therefore of houses in the *demos* is estimated at no more than 20–30 for small *demoi*, to at most 300 families/houses for the largest. Indeed, in all probability there will have been far fewer houses, if it is borne in mind that a large number of *demotai* at least one quarter of the population neither resided nor even owned property in the *demos*.

149

150

A characteristic example of this type of *demos* was Halai Aixonides, our knowledge of which is due to many years of archaeological research in Voula [fig. 158]. The settlement extended a few kilometres along the coast, between the shore and Mount Hymettos, in the form of a cloud of installations over the entire area of the *demos*. The form of the settlement was determined by two parallel roads running out of Aixone, the first along the coast and the second some 600 m further east, skirting the foothills of

151 

151 Boundary markers carved on stelai or at the foot of rocks defined the limits of sanctuaries, public or private spaces. In the Attic countryside the presence of such inscriptions on rocks is common, possibly indicating the new boundaries of the demos, as these were formed after the creation of the new Hellenistic tribes.

152 Pentele. Cave of the Nymphs. On the votive offering of Agathemeros from the cave, the Classical architectural frame has been replaced by the representation of the cave itself, locus sanctus and place of epiphany of the Nymphs, who are represented in calm interaction in the background, while Agathemeros, pouring a libation, is received by Hermes and Pan. 4th century BC. Athens, National Archaeological Museum.

Hymettos, which joined at the boundary with the neighbouring *demos* of Anagyrous, on the road to Sounion. Between these roads developed, without any particular plan, a network of minor roads bordered by dry-stone walls, houses and tomb enclosures or a small temple here and there. On the low hills to the northwest, southeast and south at Pigadakia, Voula, are three nuclei of denser settlement (at 40-m intervals), while at the south edge of the *demos*, close to the Spit of Vouliagmeni with the important sanctuary of Apollo Zoster [figs 156, 157], the fortified acropolis can be seen on the Kastraki height. Despite intensive investigations, the agora, the theatre and the public buildings that would be expected in the flat space to the north of the hill have not been found.

The excavations of the neighbouring *demoi* of Alimous, Euonymon, Aixone and Anargyrous (Vari) present a similar picture. In one other multi-nucleated settlement at the other end of Attica, at Drafi (possibly the *demos* of Teithras), which is high on the south pine-clad slopes of Vigla ton Klephton of Mount Pentele, overlooking the narrow Valanara valley, the ruins of two houses built on either side of the road have been brought to light, about 500 m apart, while further south, beside another road, the cemetery was found, with burials spanning the Geometric to the Classical period.

The inclination for some urban planning in the organization of the *demoi* in the fourth century BC, perhaps under the influence of the Hippodamean system, is borne out not only by the layout of the settlement in the fort at Sounion, but also by the characteristic appearance in all the aforementioned *demoi* of a series of independent (not incorporated in a grid) rectangular *insulae* with two (at Moschato as well as in the Mesogeia, near the Airport), three (at Voula and Pallini) or four (Thorikos) houses in which earlier buildings or towers are incorporated (Voula, Vari, Thorikos, Rhamnous). A good example of this system of *insulae* and towers can be seen in the part of the ancient *demos* of Halai Aixonides, which is preserved at the junction of Dragatsaniou and Kalymnou streets in Voula [fig. 158]. In the present case, particularly interesting is the central *insula* of the settlement, with two parallel houses of usual Athenian type with court, probably two-storeyed, which border south with a smaller house with small court and *andron*, and a circular tower (as at Thorikos and Rhamnous) in place of the *oikos*. The *insula* is surrounded by gardens and a little way to the east is a small temple. A similar complex of three parallel and virtually uniform farmhouses with court but without tower, isolated in the middle of the fields, has been uncovered in the recent excavation of the Attic Motorway (Attiki Odos) at Pallini (*demos* of Kydantidai: fig. 142).

152

153

153, 154 The aspect of 4th-century BC cemeteries in Athens, as well as in the demoi of Attica, was determined by the family tomb enclosures. The tall stele with palmette finial and the names of the dead, which was usually set up in the middle of the enclosure, was accompanied by other stelai, small temples (naiskoi) or marble vases with representations of the dead in dexioses (valediction scene) with relatives or alone, with a slave, while the corners of the enclosure were usually adorned with marble lekythoi. Discovery of the entire decoration of an enclosure in situ is rare **[see figs 146, 147]**.

Usually single reliefs are preserved, such as the illustrated grave stele with representation of a seated female figure and a female slave, of the 4th century BC, from Pallene, Panagitsa stream **[fig. 153]**. Kifissia Archaeological Museum.

A grave stele from Glyfada **[fig. 154]**. The lovely Classical figure of the woman receiving a necklace from the little nursemaid already resembles a sculpture in the round. Early 4th century BC. Piraeus Archaeological Museum.

154

155

155 Merenda. Boundary stone referring to a field with house, mortgaged against 1,500 drachmas, as surety for the dowry of a girl named Mnesistrate. Brauron Archaeological Museum.

156, 157 Vouliagmeni. Closely linked with the myth of the birth of Apollo and Artemis, the sanctuary of Apollo Zoster on the Spit of Vouliagmeni was one of the demotic sanctuaries whose reputation spread beyond the narrow boundaries of the demos. The temple had the form of a simple cella, to which a peristasis of 4x10 columns was added later.

158 Voula, ancient demos of Halai Aixonides. A complex of houses amidst gardens and narrow streets, flanked by tomb enclosures and rural sanctuaries, gives the typical picture of the Attic demos. Preserved on a large plot in Kalymnou Street, Voula.

The recent excavation at the new Equestrian Centre at Merenda, Markopoulo, where the ancient *demos* of Myrrhinous is located, gives some idea of the aspect of the centre of the aforesaid *demoi* [figs 159–163]. Here, in the middle of the flat space lying between the foothills of the homonymous mountain and the low vine-planted hills, a peripteral temple, probably dedicated to Artemis Kolainis, one of the most important in the city, and a sanctuary of Aphrodite [fig. 159] have been brought to light at the crossroad of the two central arteries of the *demos*, which are lined at intervals by cemeteries, classical tomb enclosures and two sanctuaries. Identified and excavated around the temple, at some distance, were three porticoed buildings of public character, in no particular order, the sanctuary of a phratry, which has been mentioned already, and, very close behind it, a monumental fountain that had been reconstructed in Roman times, while farmhouses extended on the small hills around.

The form of the multi-nucleated *demos* described here is characteristic of the balanced rural life of the *demoi*, in which small and medium-size properties were the norm (the values recorded on the mortgage boundary stones of the region are usually no more than 1,500 drachmas: fig. 155) and there was intensive cultivation of vines and fruit trees, which demand continuous presence and personal labour, or at least monitoring by the owner, who was assisted by one or two slaves and occasionally by neighbours. Those small agriculturalists who lived in the *Asty* went daily to their fields from there. However, even in Euonymon, which was just 35 stades (= 7.5 km) away, most *demotai* (excepting about thirty) lived on the spot and went to Athens for elections, though not the old men who could not move easily.

A different picture is presented by the *demoi* sharing the plain of the Mesogeia (Erchia, Paiania, Oe, Sphettos, Hagnous, Prospalta), where grain growing and large properties (the values on mortgage boundary stones of Erchia range between 2,000 and 6,000 drachmas) prevail. As is deduced from the portion of the first fruits (*aparchai*) of Eleusis (*Inscriptiones Graecae* II2 1672), of the Akamantis tribe (to which the last three these *demoi* belong), annual yields in grain were indeed in excess of 1,500,000 m^3 of barley and 187,000 m^3 of wheat, which means that they accounted for about one-twelfth of the production of the whole of Attica.

Representative examples of two such *demoi*, in which the cohesion of the settlement nuclei tends to be lost because of the distances between the houses, have been uncovered in the excavation occasioned by the airport at Spata, in the heart of the plain. The settlement nuclei encountered at Halai Aixonides are replaced here by some small groups of farmsteads in very sparse arrangement (over 300 m apart), which alternate with family tomb enclosures and two pottery workshops, along the side of the roads crossing the plain [figs 164, 165]. The centre is located at the intersection of the main

156

157

roads, with a community well and an open-air sanctuary. The houses are, as a rule, small with contiguous rooms [fig. 167] or just one room with upper storey, at the back of the court, without baths, androns and, primarily, without storage spaces, silos and with very few exceptions without tower, were presumably only for seasonal use or at most were dwellings of overseers, certainly not of the big landowners, who resided in Athens and were involved with politics, shipping, commerce and the mines. The harvest [fig. 170] was brought to the city, either to be stored in the cellars that are known to have existed in the mansions, such as that of the Herm-mutilators, or to be sold in the marketplace, as did the progressive Pericles.

Even greater is the dispersion of habitation in the relatively recently-colonized (post-Geometric period) regions of the *demos* of Atene and of neighbouring Amphitrope (pres. Legraina), which have been excavated systematically, or, as we have seen, of Sounion (pres. Souriza) in the Laureotike, regions with isolated farmsteads scattered in the fields, without settlement cohesion or communication. In an area of 20 sq. km. and with 126 *demotai* over 18 years of age (it elects 3 *bouleutai*), Atene is estimated to have had about 50 farmsteads (35 have already been identified) in the fourth century BC, to each of which was allotted 9 ha. of arable land. The farmsteads are at least 300–400 m apart. They are built preferably at the foot of a hill slope or at the edge of the fields, the large tower houses on high ground and at even greater distance from each other. Among them is encountered the type of small farmstead of 135–145 sq. m. known from

158

159

159 Merenda. Aerial photograph of an enclosure with garden, which has been identified as a sanctuary of Aphrodite, south of the Equestrian Centre.

160 Idyllic vista of Merenda, at the southern edge of the Mesogeia Plain (in the background), before disruption by works for the 2004 Olympic Games. The name of the area preserves a remembrance of the ancient demos of Myrrhinous, part of which was uncovered in the archaeological excavations that preceded the construction of the Equestrian Centre.

161 Merenda. Pyxis (jewellery casket) of the mature Geometric period (late 8th c. BC), from the southeast cemetery of Myrrhinous. The vase was found intact in the grave shown in fig. 163. Brauron Archaeological Museum.

162 Merenda. Aerial photograph of the worksite for the Equestrian Centre, where part of an ancient road was brought to light, leading from the demos of Myrrhinous in the direction of Paiania. On the roadside is a Classical tomb enclosure whose use continued into Roman times.

163 Merenda. Cist grave of the Geometric period, from which the pyxis [fig. 161] was recovered.

160

161

162

163

164 Spata. Large pottery workshop, active from the 4th to the 2nd century BC, in the area of Vathy Pigadi at Spata. Discernible are three kilns — two earlier rectangular ones and one later circular —, various workshop and storage facilities, as well as a row of pits for extracting clay. As was ascertained in the excavation, the workshop produced terracotta architectural members, mainly tiles and antefixes, waterspouts and beehives. The owner's name is known from a mould found in the storeroom.

165 Representation of a pottery workshop on an Attic black-figure hydria: left, the potter at the wheel, which is turned by a young man kneeling in front of it. The vases are carried carefully to the kiln, under the supervision of the owner (in the middle with stave). Munich, Antikensammlungen.

166 Acharnai. Red-figure krater of the 5th century BC, with representation of a young victor in the pentathlon and two Nikai flying towards him, to crown him with the wreath. From the area of the demos of Pergase. Menidi Archaeological Collection.

167 Spata. The ruins of a Late Classical farmstead in the northeast area of the airport at Spata. Visible are the alignment of rooms at the back of the rectangular court, the foundations of a tower next to the entrance, and the traces of a road. The twin sanctuary that was incorporated in the first room of the farmhouse dates to an earlier phase at the site (5th c. BC).

164

165

Spata. Usually, however, they are huge installations by Attic standards, up to 3,600 sq. m.(!) in some cases, with two courts, which served respectively the owner's residence, with one or even two androns, and the farmhouse, with the tower, storerooms, outbuildings and stables (for the valuable animals: *ergates bous* (draught oxen) and horses). Independently, in a radius of about 50 m, were the outdoor pens for the sheep and goats, beehives and threshing floors. Here existed farmsteads that specialized in grain growing with threshing floors up to 22 m in diameter as well as in stock raising and apiary (Attic wool as well as Attic honey were renowned), while elsewhere the presence of an oil press in the court [fig. 168] and terraces on the slope bear witness to intensive olive cultivation. The water essential for all these landholdings was supplied by wells, cisterns or by constructing small dams in adjacent streams. A similar picture is presented by some farmhouses in the Souriza valley at Sounion, spoken of above. The owners of these farmsteads, such as Timesios, known from inscriptions, or Phainippos, (Demosthenes 42.2 and 5–7) came almost exclusively from the upper echelons of society and owned estates at various places in the *demos*

166

167

168 Attica. Black-figure skyphos with representation of an oil-press. Dated to 520–510 BC. Boston, Museum of Fine Arts.

169 Athens. Red-figure amphora with representation of collecting oil extracted from the sacred olive trees of Attica, the "moriai", in the presence of Athena. As the depiction of the same vase shape in the scene indicates, this must have been its actual use. From the ancient demos of Euonymon. Piraeus Archaeological Museum.

168

or in more than one *demos*. Perhaps associated with their temporary sojourn in the countryside is the type of rural villa (*villa rustica*) with large androns, peristyle courts or *pastades*, which is attested by a series of farmhouses, such as the so-called "sacred house" at Vouliagmeni, built on high ground above the temple of Apollo Zoster and looking out to sea, or the house at Vari, in a ravine between two peaks of the outliers of Hymettos, close to the Nympholeptos cave, as well as the "Dema house" on the boundary of the Athens basin and the Thriasion plain.

The heyday enjoyed by the Attic countryside in the fourth century BC, the building boom in the *demoi* and the proliferation of demotic inscriptions, but above all the spread of cultivation to the very limits of Attica, with the large farmsteads and the endless lines of terraces covering the western slopes of Hymettos, from Alimos to Sounion, document the final turn to the land (after the failure of Athenian hegemonic ambitions). As is only natural, after securing, through imports, sufficiency of grain, there was an increasing focus on large-scale intensive cultivation, obviously with slave labour, of Attic staples (olive oil: fig. 169, wine, honey), which the big landowners were obliged to channel to the market, in order to cover their obligations to provide *choregies* and emergency contributions, through which the democratic city secured to some degree the redistribution of wealth. The now dominant presence of large land-ownership is borne out by the number of tower houses, about 50, and large wealthy farmsteads, which are the only ones (at least in Atene) that seem to survive after the fourth century BC. The measure of social inequality concealed behind the Classical democratic state of the fourth century BC is given by the property of the members of the liturgical class (that is Athenians obliged to undertake liturgies (*leitourgies* = public services). It is estimated that 7.5–9% of citizens (2,000 of the 22,000–30,000 citizens) owned over one-third to half the cultivable land (about 1,000 sq. km.) in Attica. This means that at least 24,000 ha. (according to other calculations 400 sq. km., to which is added 100 sq. km. of public land exploited through leasing), were cultivated by non-owners (most probably slaves, since there is no mention of lessees or crop-sharers), while

169

of the remaining 25,000 citizens, 8,000–15,000 medium and small farmers, who were traditionally the backbone of the democracy, barely subsisted (with 5.5–10 hectares, that is in total at most 600 sq. km.) and 5,000 were landless.

A similar economic differentiation of the population of Attica, which evolved into the antipode of the ideal Aristotelean model of a city-state based on small and medium landownership (*Economics* 11.66.26) surely had a serious impact on the settlement, social and political form of the city, and surely led to the eventual collapse of concord between *asty* and *chora*, which was the *par excellence* achievement of Kleisthenian isonomy. The new opportunities for employing or subsidizing the landless, which the maritime empire provided, had led early on to the gradual shift of the centre of gravity from the rural to the urban economy, the concentration of *demotai* and of money in Athens and the new *asty* of the Piraeus. Thus, the differentiation between city-dwellers and countryfolk gradually acquired social dimensions, stressing pre-existing cultural ones. However, the breakdown of the concord between *asty* and *chora* was not completed before the Hellenistic period (330–146 BC), when the concentration of land [fig. 171] and the distance between the Athenian burghers and the peasants (*agroikoi*), hinted at in Aristophanes' *Clouds* (134ff.), took on a political form, with the exclusion of the latter from the State. And so we come to the traveller Herakleides (3rd century BC), who to the noble, generous and open Athenians juxtaposes, as a different race of men, the busy, garrulous and suspicious inhabitants of Attica.

170

171

170 Merenda. Lead stathmon (state-approved balance weight) with representation of a tortoise, from Myrrhinous. Brauron Archaeological Museum.

171 Spata. The ruins of one of the two farmsteads of the Hellenistic period (4th-mid–2nd c. BC), which were excavated in the area of the airport at Spata. The extent, the large number of spaces and the rarity of Hellenistic farmsteads are characteristic of the concentration of land-ownership in the hands of a few.

Piraeus

GEORGE STEINHAUER

The very rapid development of the Kleisthenian *demos* of the Piraeus, of whose original form no trace survives, into a second *asty*, the naval station of the maritime empire and the centre of Mediterranean trade, is due to Themistocles' decision (493 BC) to transfer the port of Athens to the barren Peiraike Peninsula, isolated behind the marshlands of the Kephissos but provided with three good harbours [fig. 25]. In the early years after the Persian Wars, the Piraeus was still no more than a fortified promontory lapped by the sea, where the old fort loomed high above the circular military harbours of Zea and Mounichia, and the very ancient temple of Artemis Mounichia dominated the edge of the small harbour. Nonetheless, the city grew rapidly, reaching Athens shortly before the Peloponnesian War. Its population of 20,000–30,000, for the most part alien to the *demos*, was made up of citizens of other *demoi* and metics [fig. 172], Greeks and foreigners (Isocrates, *On The Peace* 2.21), whose activities were closely almost exclusively bound with the two pillars of the Athenian imperialist democracy, the fleet and commerce. Among them the "*nautikos ochlos*" (maritime mob) of serving oarsmen, captains, merchants and middlemen held first place, which primarily benefited from the maritime empire. This fact explains the distrust or even the hostility with which the Piraeus was treated by the conservative Athenians, such as Plato in *Gorgias* (518e–519a), for whom the foundation of the state was not the walls and the fleet, but the people of the Attic *demoi*.

The particular importance of the "twin" city is underlined by the fact that in 404 BC the Thirty Tyrants appointed *ten archons of the Piraeus*, that the city's *demarchos* was appointed by the state by drawing lot, and that to him were intended half the *astynomoi* (magistrates responsible for policing the city), *metronomoi* (magistrates responsible for weights and measures) and *sitophylakes* (grain inspectors) that the city appointed annually. The spirit underlying the founding of the Piraeus also prevailed in its rationalist layout, around 470–460 BC, by the father and theoretician of urban planning, Hippodamos of Miletos. With the almost contemporary creation, between 458/7 and 446/5 BC, of the 180 m-wide fortified corridor of the Long Walls,

172

172 Piraeus. Grave stele of the metic Diogenes son of Apollonis, from Pyrrha on Lesbos (4th c. BC). It was found in front of the Eetioneia Gate of the Piraeus. The rare preservation of the blue ground, on which one painted lilly can be discerned, helps our appreciation of the use of colour in enhancing the figure in ancient sculpture. Piraeus Archaeological Museum.

173

173 Piraeus. One of the boundary stones, possibly of the Hippodamean agora of the Piraeus. Before the mid-5th century BC. Piraeus Archaeological Museum.

174 Piraeus. Part of the excellently preserved seawall of the Piraeus, as built in 394 BC by Konon, surrounding the entire Peiraike Peninsula.

sections of which survive next to the tracks of the electric railway at Neo Faliro and Moschato, the two cities constituted one solid fortress, impregnable from the land, of a now maritime empire [fig. 174].

The fortification walls (particularly the seawalls), the two gates inside and outside of the Long Walls [figs 41, 175], which led to Athens, and the Eetioneia Gate [fig. 176], still stand in very good condition. This is not the case with the monuments of the Naval Station and the Emporion. Of the enormous utilitarian and therefore no less monumental constructions of the ancient Naval Station, which gave the Zea harbour its distinctive buildings that came to be admired as works on a par with the Acropolis monuments (Demosthenes, *Against Androtion* 22.76), the Skeuotheke of Philon was identified in 1988, with the help of the well-known inscription recording the architect's detailed specifications [fig. 177]. This is a huge storehouse 130 m long for the sails, ropes and tackle of the trieremes. The monumental shipsheds (*neosoikoi*) for the same trieremes, divided by colonnades into pairs of parallel compartments under a pitched roof, were visible years ago, half-submerged due to the rise in sea level [figs 178, 179]. Today they survive in fragmentary state in basements on the waterfront of Pashalimani and Tourkolimano. Even fewer are the visible ruins of the Emporion, the commercial zone of the central harbour of Kantharos, which extended the length of present Akti Miaouli from Karaiskaki Square to the Customs House, and was delimited by a defensive wall and a boundary stone. Of the two lighthouses, columns topped by a beacon that marked from afar the entrance to the harbour, the north one is preserved in the fertilizer factory, the south in the Maritime Administration of the Aegean, restored next to the enclosure that is identified with the tomb of Themistocles. However, the Emporion itself has disappeared, due to the rise in sea level and the construction of the quay, which, very soon after the transfer of the capital of the new Greek Kingdom to Athens, covered the remains of the ancient jetties and the buildings that are recognized in earlier drawings. In Antiquity its monumental aspect was determined by the *diazeugma*, the wide mole exactly in the middle of the shore, and the five large stoas, known of from the scholia on Aristophanes' *Peace* (line 145). Only scant traces of the stoas and of the enceinte of the commercial zone survive, in the mire of the sunken harbour and under the foundations of Late Roman buildings. Better known is the *Makra* (= Long, 200 m in length) or *Alphitopolis Stoa*, where rations of barley flour were distributed to the crews, before the fleet set sail, and to the *demos* in the event of failed harvests. Its ruins were identified recently at the corner of Akti Poseidonos and Gounari Street, at the north end of the Emporion, very close to the fortification wall. The importance of the grain trade, on which the survival of Athens largely depended, is borne out by the number of grain-cargo ships (estimated at six) that unloaded each day in

174

175

the harbour, while from around 430 BC there is a detailed description by Hermippos (Athenaeus, *Deipnosophistae* I.27e-f) of the diversity of goods-worthy of any modern consumer city that flowed into the Piraeus from everywhere.The layout of the city of Piraeus is the only known work by the urban-planner Hippodamos, who here proceeded to formulate an integrated philosophical thesis on the rational organization of the life of the *polis* and on the materialization of the idea of isonomy in urban space, so that the Piraeus would be a living lesson of cogent planning, human measure and democratic equality. The theoretical basis of Hippodamos' successful plan was the conscientious application of the Pythagorean theory of numbers in the layout of the streets and the open spaces, the harmonious proportions of which result in the sense of serene well-being given by musical harmony and classical art in general. The rational arrangement of the communal spaces, with the basic separation and the clear demarcation with boundary stones of public, private and sacred spaces (the Naval Station, the Emporion, the agora, the sanctuaries and the residential neighbourhoods) created the preconditions for the smooth running of the city [fig. 173]. On the other hand, the design of the typical Piraean house, 20.31x11.87 m in area, with central court at the far end of which, behind the porch (*prostas*), were the main rooms, the *andron* and the *oikos*, put into practice the principal of isonomy.

Thus, the building *insulae* in the Piraeus, some of which can now be visited [figs 181, 182], were divided initially into eight plots in two rows of four plots of 240 sq.m. The situation changed in the Hellenistic period [fig. 180], when, with accumulation of properties, large houses with atria and

176

175 Piraeus. The Asty Gate, inside of the corridor of the Long Walls, was flanked by two circular towers (diam. 10m). The court served to trap the enemy.

176 Piraeus. The recently restored gateway of the Eetioneia fort, which controlled the north side of the large harbour. Visible in front is the moat with the two posts of the wooden drawbridge

177 Piraeus. The foundations of the north entrance to the Skeuotheke of Philon, at 170 Ypsilantou Street. One other part of the skeuotheke, which was up to 130 m long, was found on the roadbed of Merarchias Street. Identification of the monument was possible, thanks to the very detailed specifications of the architect, recorded in an inscription found in 1898.

178 Piraeus. The ruins of the ship-sheds (neosoikoi) of the Zea harbour, on the east side of Pashalimani, as these survived in the late 19th century, before construction of the coast road.

179 Piraeus. Reconstruction of the ship-sheds (neosoikoi) of Zea, according to the study by the Danish Archaeological Institute (drawing by I. Nakas)

177

178

179

180

181

182

other appointments were built. Streets of different width (5 m and 8 m) separated the *insulae* and the quarters respectivelyrespectively , while wide thoroughfares (15 m) connected the major sectors (Emporion, Naval Station, Agora) with one another and with the entrances to the city. In the absence of wells, water was supplied through a well-devised system of cisterns, while there was a full drainage system along the sides of the streets. The bland uniformity of this ideal plan was relieved by the marketplaces and the sanctuaries [fig. 183], but mainly by the varied outline of the coasts and the undulating terrain of the peninsula, which necessitated building on terraces, as for example on the slopes of Mounichia hill. Thus, it is by no means strange that the Piraeus, so admired by its contemporaries, was the model for the Hellenistic and Roman city, which was by then alienated from its rural territory.

183

180 Piraeus. The little Hellenistic theatre of Zea, in the courtyard of the Archaeological Museum, is a small-scale copy of the Lykourgean Theatre of Dionysos in Athens. The Classical theatre of Dionysos in the Piraeus, which was identified in the late 19th century on the slopes of Mounichia hill, has been lost.

181 Piraeus. Ancient building insula in Iroon Polytechneiou Street.

182 Piraeus. Ancient building insula in Terpsithea Square.

183 Piraeus. In the pose and gaze of the larger than life-size "Piraeus Athena", of the 4th century BC, the Late Classical change in the concepts of the Pheidian Athena Parthenos can be discerned. This is one of five bronze statues discovered in 1959, in an ancient warehouse close the harbour. Piraeus Archaeological Museum.

Bibliography

GENERAL BIBLIOGRAPHY

Bouras Ch. et al. (eds), *Athens: From the Classical Period to the Present Day (5th Century B.C.–A.D. 2000)*, Athens 2000.

Camp J.M., *The Archaeology of Athens*, New Haven 2001.

Coulson W.D.E. et al. (eds), *The Archaeology of Athens and Attica under the Democracy*, Oxford 1994.

Der neue Pauly. Enzyclopaedie der Antike. Altertum, Band 2, Stuttgart-Weimar 168–195 s.v. Athenai (H.R. Goette).

Doga-Toli M. – St. Oikonomou (eds), *Αρχαιολογικές Συμβολές Α: Αττική*, Museum of Cycladic Art, Athens 2013.

Doumas C. (ed.), *Mesogaia: History and Culture of Mesogeia in Attica*, Athens 2001.

Eickstedt von K.-V., *Beiträge zur Topographie des antiken Piraeus*, Athens 1991.

Étienne R., *Athènes. Espaces urbain et histoire. Des origins à la fin du IIIe siècle ap. J.-C.*, Paris 2004.

Ficuciello L., *Le strade di Atene*, Atene - Paestum 2008.

Goette H.R., J. Hammerstaedt, *Das antike Athen*, München 2004.

Goette H.R., *Ο αξιόλογος δήμος Σούνιον. Landeskundliche Studien in Südost-Attika*, Athen 2000.

Jones N.F., *Rural Athens under Democracy*, Philadelphia 2004.

Kakavogianni O. (ed.), *Αρχαιολογικές έρευνες στην Μερέντα Μαρκοπούλου*, Athens 2003.

Kakavogiannis E., "Μέταλλα εργάσιμα και συγκεχωρημένα. Η οργάνωση της εκμετάλλευσης του ορυκτού πλούτου της Λαυρεωτικής από την Αθηναϊκή Δημοκρατία", *Δημοσιεύματα-Αρχαιολογικό Δελτίο* 90, ΥΠΠΟ, Αθήνα 2005.

Korres M. (ed.), *Αττικής οδοί. Οι δρόμοι της Αττικής*, Athens 2009.

Lambrinoudakis V.K., *Οικοδομικά προγράμματα στην αρχαία Αθήνα. 479–431 π.Χ.*, Athens 1986.

Mastrapas A., *Η πόλις και το άστυ των Αθηνών*, Athens 2003.

Pantelidou M., *Αἱ προϊστορικαὶ Ἀθῆναι*, Athens 1975.

Papachatzis N.D., *Παυσανίου Αττικά*, Athens 1974.

Petrakos V.Ch., *Ο Δήμος του Ραμνούντος*, Athens 1999.

Salliora-Oikonomakou M., *Ο Αρχαίος δήμος του Σουνίου*, Athens 2004.

Solders S., *Die ausserstädtischen Kulte und die Einigung Attikas*, Lund 1931.

Travlos J., *Bildlexikon zur Topographie des antiken Attika*, Tübingen 1988.

Travlos J., *Pictorial Dictionary of Ancient Athens*, New York 1971.

Travlos I., *Πολεοδομικὴ ἐξέλιξις τῶν Ἀθηνῶν*, Athens 1960 (reprint 1993).

Vasilopoulou V. – St. Katsarou-Tzeveleki (eds), *Από τα Μεσόγεια στον Αργοσαρωνικό, Το έργο της Β' Εφορείας Προϊστορικών και Κλασικών Αρχαιοτήτων τη δεκαετία 1994-2003*, Athens 2009.

PREHISTORIC TIMES

Benzi M., *Ceramica Micenea in Attica*, Milano 1975.

Darcque P., "Les vestiges mycéniens découverts sous le Télestérion d'Eleusis", *Bulletin de Correspondance Hellénique* 105, 1981, 593–605.

Iakovidis S., *Περατή. Τὸ νεκροταφεῖον*, Athens 1969–1970.

Immerwahr S., *The Neolithic and Bronze Ages. The Athenian Agora* XIII, Princeton 1971.

Kakavogianni O., "Ο Πρωτοελλαδικός οικισμός στο Κορωπί και η μελέτη της Πρωτοελλαδικής Αττικής", in *Πρακτικά Γ' Επιστημονικής Συνάντησης ΝΑ Αττικής*, Kalyvia 1988, 321–336.

Kakavogianni O. – K. Douni – Ph. Nezeri, «Silver Metallurgical Finds dating from the end of the Final Neolithic period until the Middle Bronze Age in the area of Mesogeia», in I. Tzachili (ed.), *Aegean Metallurgy in the Bronze Age, Proceedings of an International symposium held at the University of Crete, Rethymnon, Greece, on November 19-21, 2004*, Athens, 2008, 45–57.

Kakavogiannis E., "Μυκηναϊκό νεκροταφείο στο λόφο Φούρεσι του δήμου των Γλυκών Νερών Αττικής", *Αρχαιολογικά Ανάλεκτα εξ Αθηνών* 32–34, 1999–2001, 55–70.

Lambert N. et al., *La grotte préhistorique de Kitsos (Attique)*, Paris 1981.

Lauter H., *Kiapha Thiti, Ergebnisse der Augrabungen* II.1. *Die bronzezeitliche Architektur, Marburger Winckelmann-Programm* 1996 (2000).

Maran J., *Kiapha Thiti, Ergebnisse der Ausgrabungen* II 2 (2.Jt.v. Chr.: *Keramik und Kleinfunde*), Marburg 1992.

Mussche H., *Thorikos. A Guide to the Excavations*, Brussels 1974.

Mylonas G., *Τὸ Δυτικὸ νεκροταφεῖο τῆς Ἐλευσίνος*, Athens 1975.

Mylonas G., *Aghios Kosmas. An Early Bronze Age Settlement and Cemetery in Attica*, Princeton 1959.

Pantelidou-Gofa M., *Ἡ Νεολιθικὴ Νέα Μάκρη. Τὰ οἰκοδομικά*, Athens 1991.

Pantelidou-Gofa M., *Ἡ Νεολιθικὴ Νέα Μάκρη. Ἡ κεραμεική*, Athens 1995.

Pantelidou M., *Ἡ νεολιθικὴ Ἀττική*, Athens 1997.

Pantelidou-Gofa M., *Τὸ πρωτοελλαδικὸ νεκροταφεῖο στὸ Τσέπι Μαραθῶνος*, Athens 2004.

Papadopoulos Th. – L. Kontorli-Papadopoulou, *Vravron. The Mycenaean cemetery, Studies in Mediterranean Archaeology* 142, Uppsala 2014.

Papathanassopoulos G. (ed.), *Neolithic Culture in Greece*, Athens 1996.

Sgouritsa-Polychronakou N., "Το μυκηναϊκό νεκροταφείο της Βάρκιζας/Βάρης", *Αρχαιολογική Δελτίο* 43, 1988, Μελέτες, 1–108.

Sgouritsa-Polychronakou N., "Η μυκηναϊκή εγκατάσταση στο Βουρβάτσι", *Αρχαιολογικό Δελτίο* 56, 2001, Μελέτες, 1–82.

Steinhauer G., "The Attiki Odos from the Stavros intersection to the Leontari and Pallini intersection", in G. Steinhauer (ed.), *Attiki Odos: an ancient footpath, a modern highway*, Athens 2005, 158–163.

Theocharis D., "Ἀσκηταριό. Πρωτοελλαδικὴ ἀκρόπολις παρὰ τὴν Ραφήναν", *Αρχαιολογικὴ Εφημερίς* 1953–4, vol. 92–93, part C, 59–76.

Theocharis D., G. Mylonas, S. Iakovidis, *Ιστορία του Ελληνικού Έθνους*, vol. I, "Προϊστορία και Πρωτοϊστορία", Athens 1971.

Wright J. – N. Sgouritsa – N. Papadimitriou – S. Fachard, *Athens and Attica in Prehistory*. Proceedings of the international conference held at Athens, 27-31 May 2015 (Athens), forthcoming.

HISTORICAL TIMES

Bengtson H., *History of Greece from the Beginnings to the Byzantine Era* (translated by E.F. Bloedow), Ottawa 1988.

Brenne St., "Ostraka and the Process of Ostrakophoria", in W. D. E. Coulson, O. Palagia et al. (eds), *The Archaeology of Athens and Attica under Democracy, Oxbow Monograph* 37, Oxford 1994, 13–24.

Bury B. – R. Meiggs, *A History of Greece*, London 1975[4].

Habicht Chr., *Athens from Alexander to Antony* (translated by D. L. Schneider), Cambridge (Mass.) 1997.

Hall J.M., *A History of the Archaic Greek World (ca 1200–479 BC)*, Oxford 2007.

Kroll J.H., "An Archive of the Athenian Cavalry", *Hesperia* 46, 1977, 83–140.

Lang M.L., *The Athenian Agora* XXI. *Graffiti and Dipinti*, Princeton 1976.

Lang M.L., *The Athenian Agora* XXV. *Ostraka*, Princeton 1990.

Matthaiou A.P., "Ἡρίον Λυκούργου Λυκόφρονος Βουτάδου", *ΗΟΡΟΣ* 5, 1987, 31–44.

Matthaiou A.P., "Νέος λίθος τοῦ μνημείου μὲ τὰ ἐπιγράμματα γιὰ τοὺς Περσικοὺς πολέμους", *ΗΟΡΟΣ* 6, 1988, 118–122.

Matthaiou A.P., "Ἀθηναίοισι τεταγμένοισι ἐν τεμένεϊ Ἡρακλέος" (Hdt. 6.108.1), in P. Derow, R. Parker (eds), *Herodotus and his World. Essays from a Conference in Memory of George Forrest*, Oxford 2003, 190–202.

Matthaiou A.P., "Εἰς Agora I 4256", *ΗΟΡΟΣ* 14–16, 2003, 143–152.

Matthaiou A.P., "Attic Public Inscriptions of the Fifth Century BC in Ionic Script", in L. Mitchell, L. Rubinstein (eds), *Greek History and Epigraphy in Honour of P. J. Rhodes*, Swansea 2009, 201-212.

Meiggs R. – D. Lewis, *A Selection of Greek Historical Inscriptions to the End of the Fifth Century BC*, Oxford 1988.

Rhodes P.J. – R. Osborne, *Greek Historical Inscriptions 403–323 B.C.*, Oxford 2003.

Rhodes P.J., *A History of the Classical Greek World (478–323 BC)*, Oxford 2006.

Siewert P. (ed.), *Ostrakismos - Testimonien* I (*Historia Einzelschriften* 155), Stuttgart 2002.

Sironen E., *The Late Roman and Early Byzantine Inscriptions of Athens and Attica*, Helsinki 1997.

Stroud R.S., "An Athenian Law on Silver Coinage", *Hesperia* 43, 1974, 157–188.

Stroud R.S., *The Athenian Grain-Tax Law of 374/3 B.C., Hesperia*, Suppl. 29, Princeton 1998.

Thompson H.A. – R.E. Wycherley, *The Athenian Agora* XIV. *The Agora of Athens*, Princeton 1972.

Tod M.N., *A Selection of Greek Historical Inscriptions to the End of the Fifth Century BC*, Oxford 1946[2].

Tod M.N., *A Selection of Greek Historical Inscriptions*, vol. II. *From 403 to 323 BC*, Oxford 1948.

ATHENS

Αρχαιολογία της πόλης των Αθηνών (publ. National Hellenic Research Foundation, Athens 1996).

Connolly P. – H. Dodge, *The Ancient City: Life In Classical Athens And Rome*. Oxford-New York, 1998.

Greco E. et al., *Topografia di Atene. Sviluppo urbano e monumenti dalle origini al III secolo d.C.*, vol. 1-5, Atene - Paestum 2010-2015.

Parlama L. – N. Stampolidis (eds), *The City Beneath the City. Finds from Excavations for the Metropolitan Railway of Athens*, Athens 2000.

For Athens in the Archaic period

Queyrel A., *Athènes. La cité archaique et classique du VIIIe s. à la fin du Ve s.*, Paris 2003.

For Athens in the Classical period

Roberts J.W., *City of Socrates. An Introduction to Classical Athens*, London 1984.

Samons L.J. (ed.), *The Cambridge Companion to the Age of Pericles*, Cambridge 2007.

For Athens in the 4th century BC

Knell H., *Athen im 4. Jh. v. Chr. Eine Stadt veraendert ihr Gesicht*, Darmstadt 2000.

For Athens in the Hellenistic period

Habicht Chr., *Athen. Die Geschichte der Stadt in hellenistischer Zeit*, München 1995.

Palagia O. – St. V. Tracy (eds), Proceedings of the Symposium: *The Macedonians in Athens. 322–229 B.C.*, Oxford 2003.

For Athens in Roman times

Castren P. (ed.), *Post-Herulian Athens. Aspects of Life and Culture in Athens, AD 267–529*, Helsinki 1994.

Follet S., *Athènes au IIe et an IIIe siècle*, Paris 1979.

Hoff M. – S. Rotroff, *The Romanisation of Athens*, Oxford 1997.

For the Acropolis

Holtzmann B., *L'Acropole d'Athènes*, Paris 2003.

Hurwit J. M., *The Athenian Acropolis. History, Mythology and Archaeology from the Neolithic Era to the Present*, Cambridge-New York 1999.

Hurwit J. M., *The Acropolis in the Age of Pericles*, Cambridge-New York 2004.

Korres M. et al., *The Parthenon, Architecture and Conservation*, Athens 1999.

Korres M., "The History of the Acropolis Monuments", in R. Economakis (ed.), *Acropolis Restoration. The CCAM Interventions*, London 1994.

Rhodes R. F., *Architecture and Meaning on the Athenian Acropolis*, Cambridge 1995.

For the Ancient Agora

Camp J.M., *The Athenian Agora: A Short Guide to the Excavations*, Athens 2003.

Mauzy C.A., *Οι ανασκαφές στην Αγορά της Αθήνας. 1931–2006. Εικονογραφημένο ιστορικό*, Athens 2006.

Ober J. – Ch. Hedrick (eds), *The Birth of Democracy*, Princeton 1993.

SANCTUARIES OF ATTICA

Baumer L.E., *Kult im Kleinen. Ländliche Heiligtümer spätarchaischer bis hellenistischer Zeit. Attika-Arkadien-Argolis-Kynouria*, Rahden/Westf. 2004.

Burkert W., *Ελληνική μυθολογία και τελετουργία* (Greek transl.), Athens 1993.

Burkert W., *Griechische Religion der archaischen und klassischen Epoche*, Stuttgart-Berlin-Köln-Mainz 2010[2].

Deubner L., *Attische Feste*, Berlin 1966[2].

Hamilton R., *Choes and Anthesteria. Athenian Iconography and Ritual*, Ann Arbor 1992.

Jones N.F., *The Associations of Classical Athens, The Responses to Democracy*, New York-Oxford 1999.

Kaltsas N. – Shapiro A. (eds), *Worshiping Women. Ritual and Reality in Classical Athens*, Athens, 2008.

Lalonde G.V., *HOROS DIOS, An Athenian Shrine and Cult of Zeus*, Leiden 2006.

Mersch A., *Studien zur Siedlungsgeschichte Attikas von 950 bis 400 v. Chr.*, Frankfurt 1996.

Mikalson J., *Religion in Hellenistic Athens*, Berkeley 1998.

Palaiokrassa L. – E. Vivliodetis, "The Sanctuaries of Artemis Mounichia and Zeus Parnessios", in V. Vlachou (ed.), *Pots, Workshops and Early Iron Age Society: Function and Role of Ceramics in Early Greece, Proceedings of the International Symposium held at the Université libre de Bruxelles, 14-16 November 2013*, Bruxelles 2015, 155–180.

Parke H.W., *Festivals of the Athenians*, Ithaca 1977.

Parker R., *Athenian Religion. A History*, Oxford 2004².

Parker R., *Polytheism and Society at Athens*, Oxford 2005.

Papangeli K., *Ελευσίνα. Ο αρχαιολογικός χώρος και το Μουσείο*, Athens 2002.

Simon E., *Festivals of Attica: An Archaeological Commentary*, Madison 1983.

Sourvinou-Inwood Chr., *Tragedy and Athenian Religion*, Oxford 2003.

Sourvinou-Inwood Chr., *Athenian Myths and Festivals* (ed. R. Parker), New York 2010.

ATTIC *DEMOI*

Adreyev V.N., "Some Aspects of Agrarian Conditions in Attica in the Fifth to Third Centuries B.C.", *Eirene* 12, 1974, 19.

Andreou I., "Ο δήμος των Αιξωνίδων Αλών", in W.D. Coulson, O. Palagia et al. (eds), *The Archaeology of Athens and Atttica under the Democracy, Oxbow Monograph* 37, Oxford 1994, 191–215.

Davies J.K., *The Athenian Propertied Families*, Oxford 1971.

de Ste Croix G., "The Estate of Phainippus", in E. Badian (ed.), *Ancient Society and Institutions: Studies Presented to Victor Ehrenberg*, Oxford 1966, 109–111.

Eliot C.W.J., *Coastal Demes of Attica. A Study of the Policy of Kleisthenes*, Toronto 1962.

Foxhall L., "The Control of the Attic Landscape. Agriculture in Ancient Greece", in B. Wells (ed.), *Agriculture in Ancient Greece, 16–17 May 1990*, Stockholm 1992, 155–159.

Goette H.R., "Sounion III: eine klassische Farm über dem Souriza-Tal", *Athenische Mitteilungen* 110, 1995, 182–205.

Hansen M.H., *Demography and Democracy. The Number of Athenian Citizens in the Fourth Century BC*, Herning 1985, 51–64.

Hoepfner W., *Geschichte des Wohnens* I, *5000 v. Chr. - 500 v. Chr.*, Stuttagrt 1999, 245–260.

Jones J. E., "Town and Country Houses of Attica in Classical Times", *Miscellanea Graeca* 1, 1975, 63–139.

Kaza K., "Ευώνυμον και Αλιμούς", *Άλιμος, Όψεις της ιστορίας της πόλης και του δήμου*, Athens 16–151.

Konsolaki E., *Γλυφάδα. Ιστορικόν παρελθόν και μνημεία*, Athens 1990.

Lambert S.D., *The Phratries of Attica*, Michigan 1993.

Langdon M.K., "The Topography of Coastal Erechtheis", *Chiron* 18, 1988, 43–54.

Lohmann H., *Atene, Ατήνη. Forschungen zur Siedlungs- und Wirtschaftsstuktur des klassischen Attika*, Köln-Weimar-Wien 1993.

Mikalson J.D., "Religion in the Attic Demes", *American Journal of Philology* 98, 1977, 424–435.

Millett P., "Patronage and its Avoidance in Ancient Athens", in A. Wallace-Hadrill (ed.), *Patronage in Ancient Society*, London 1989, 15–47.

Mussche H. et al. (eds), *Thorikos* IX 145, 1977–82, 145 (Bingen).

Mussche H., *Thorikos, A Mining Town in Ancient Attika*, Gent 1998.

Osborne R., *Demos. The Discovery of Classical Attica*, Cambridge 1985.

Osborne R., "Buildings and Residence on the Land in Classical and Hellenistic Greece. The Contribution of Epigraphy", *Annual of the British School at Athens* 80, 1985, 119–128.

Osborne R., *Classical Landscape with Figures. The Ancient Greek City and his Countryside*, London 1987.

Osborne R., "'Is it a Farm?' The Definition of Agricultural Sites and Settlements in Ancient Greece", in B. Wells (ed.), *Agriculture in Ancient Greece. Proceedings of the Seventh International Symposium at the Swedish Institute at Athens, 16–17 May 1990*, Stockholm 1992, 21–25.

Perrin E., "Herakleides le Crétois à Athènes, Les plaisirs du toutisme culturel", *Revue des Études Grecques* 107, 1994, 192–202.

Pritchett W., "The Attic Stelai. Part I", *Hesperia* 22, 1953, 225–229; "Part 2", *Hesperia* 25, 1956, 178–317. The most recent finds: *Inscriptiones Graecae* I³, 421–430.

Roy C., "Demosthenes 50 as Evidence for Isolated Farmsteads in Classical Attica", *Liverpool Classical Monthly* 13,4 (April 1998), 57.

Salliora-Oikonomakou M., " Ἀρχαία ἀγορὰ στὸ λιμάνι Πασᾶ Λαυρίου", *Αρχαιολογικό Δελτίο* 34, 1979, Μελέτες, 161–173.

Siewert P., *Die Trittyen Attikas und die Heeresreform des Kleisthenes*, München 1982.

Stanton G.R., "Some Inscriptions in ATTIC DEMES", *Annual of the British School at Athens* 91, 1996, 341–364.

Steinhauer G., "Παρατηρήσεις στην οικιστική μορφή των αττικών δήμων", in W. D. Coulson – O. Palagia et al. (eds), *The Archaeology of Athens and Atttica under the Democracy, Oxbow Monograph* 37, 1994, 175–189.

Steinhauer G., *The Archaeological Museum of Piraeus*, Athens 2001.

Steinhauer G., "The Classical Mesogaia (5th–4th century BC)", I. The Kleisthenian demes. Road network and settlement pattern in the Classical Mesogaia, in C. Doumas (ed.), *Mesogaia: History and Culture of Mesogeia in Attica*, Athens 2001, 81–153 (with bibliography).

Steinhauer G., *Marathon and the Archaeological Museum*, Athens 2009.

Traill J., *The Political Organization of Attica, Hesperia*, Suppl. 14, 1975, *Demos and Trittys, Epigraphical and Topographical Studies in the Organization of Attica*, Toronto 1986.

Whitehead D., *The Demes of Attica 508/7- ca 250 BC*, Princeton 1986.

Wood E.M., "Agricultural Slavery in Classical Athens", *American Journal of Archaeology* 8, 1983, 1–46.

Wood E.M., *Peasant Citizen and Slave. The Foundations of Athenian Democracy*, London-New York 1988.

PIRAEUS

Garland R., *The Piraeus from the Fifth to the First Century BC*, New York 1987.

Hoepfner W. – E.L. Schwandner, *Haus und Stadt im klassischen Griechenland Neubearbeitung*, München 1994, 22–50.

Steinhauer G., "Ancient Piraeus, the city of Themistocles and Hippodamos", in *Piraeus, Centre of Shipping and Culture*, Athens 2000, 10–123.

KNEMIS
VARDOUSIA MOUNTAINS
CHLO
MANMADE LAKE MORNOS
PHOKIS
RIVER KEPHISSOS
GULF OF ITEA
HELIK
MA
CORINTHIAN GULF
ALKYONI ISLAND
Perac
Greece
PELOPONNESE

AEGEAN SEA
KANTILI/ MAKISTOS
NORTH EUBOEAN GULF
EUBOEA
DIRPHYS
RIVER LELAS
LAKE PARALIMNI
LAKE YLIKI
BOEOTIA
Oropos
SOUTH EUBOEAN GULF
Hysaiai
Plataies/Plataiai
Kriekouki/Frythrai
Dryos Kephalai
KITHAIRON
Eleutherai
Panakton
PARNES
Sanctuary of Zeus
Aphidnai
Rhamnus
MANMADE LAKE MARATHON
Porto Germeno/Aigosthena
Cave of Pan
Oinoe
Vranas
Tsepi
Lychnospilia
Plasi
Ereneia
Kryphtis
Aglos Ioannis
Vathychoria
Agreliki/Marathon
Cemetery of Pagai
ATTICA
PENTELE
Nea Makri
Aris
MEGARIS
Orgas
Cave of Nymphs
Mazi
Kynosoura
Eleusis
Tholos tomb at Menidi
Tripodiskos
Trikerato
Rafina
Askitario
Zeus Aphesios
Megara
Rizoupolis Cave
PETALIOI ISLETS
Skironides
Nisaia
Daphni
Pallini
Palaiokastro
Minoa
RIVER KEPHISSOS
Leontari cave
Glyka Nera
Zagani
Loutsa
Athens
Sanctuary of Zeus
Spata
SALAMIS
Piraeus
HYMETTOS
Brauron
Koropi
Pousi Kalogeri
Sphettos
Perati
Steiria
Agios Kosmas
Vari
Lambrika
Merenda/Myrhinous
Raftis Islet
Lamptrai
Markopoulo
Prasiai
Glyphada
SARONIC GULF
Voula
Kiafa Thiti
Kerateas Cave
Varkiza
PANI
Kephali
AEGINA
Thorikos
Lavrion/Laureion
ANGISTRI
Agios Nikolaos
Kitsos Cave
MAKRONISOS

PHOTO CREDITS

1. Photographic Archive II EPCA (photo. V. von Eickstedt) • 2. Photographic Archive O. Kakavogianni • 3. Reproduced from M. Pantelidou, *Neolithic Attica*, Athens 1997, fig. 31 • 4. Photographic Archive II EPCA (photo. C. Xenikakis) • 5. Photographic Archive Merenda Excavations, II EPCA • 6. Photographic Archive O. Kakavogianni (photo. V. von Eickstedt) • 7. Photographic Archive II EPCA (photo. N. Daniilidis) • 8. Photographic Archive M. Pantelidou Gofa • 9. Photo. A. Vlachopoulos • 10–12. Photographic Archive NAM (photo. I. Miari) • 13. Photographic Archive II EPCA (photo. E. Banou) • 14. Photographic Archive Belgian Archaeological School • 15. Photographic Archive E. Kakavogiannis (photo. V. von Eickstedt) • 16. Photographic Archive II EPCA (photo. Y. Patrikianos) • 17a. Photographic Archive NAM (photo. I. Miari) • 17b. Photographic Archive NAM (photo. Y. Patrikianos) • 18. Photographic Archive NAM (photo. Y. Patrikianos) • 19. Photographic Archive Archaeological Society at Athens • 20. Photographic Archive NAM (photo. Y. Patrikianos) • 21. Photographic Archive NAM (photo. I. Miari) • 22. Photographic Archive Staatliche Antikensammlungen, Munich • 23. Photographic Archive Museum of Fine Arts, Boston • 24. Photographic Archive Epigraphic Museum • 25. Photo. N. Daniilidis • 26. Photographic Archive Epigraphic Museum • 27. Photographic Archive Epigraphic Museum • 28. Photographic Archive Ancient Agora Excavations • 29. Photographic Archive Epigraphic Museum • 30. Photographic Archive NAM, drawing Th. Kakarouga (photo. V. von Eickstedt) • 31. Photographic Archive MELISSA Publishing House (photo. E. Eliades) • 32. Photographic Archive II EPCA • 34. Photographic Archive A.P. Matthaiou (photo. III EPCA) • 35a–c. Reproduced from S. Brenne, 'Ostraka and the Process of Ostrakophoria', in W.D.E. Coulson, O. Palagia, et allii (eds), *The Archaeology of Athens and Attica under Democracy*, Oxford 1994, 13–24 • 36. Photographic Archive Epigraphic Museum • 37, 38. Photographic Archive Ancient Agora Excavations • 39. Photo. G. Kouroupis • 40. Photographic Archive Ancient Agora Excavations • 41. Photographic Archive XXXVI EPCA • 42, 43. Photographic Archive Epigraphic Museum • 44. Photographic Archive Museum of the Ancient Agora • 45. Photo. G. Kouroupis • 46. Photographic Archive A.P. Matthaiou (photo. III EPCA) • 47. Photographic Archive Ancient Agora Excavations • 48. Photographic Archive Epigraphic Museum • 49. Photographic Archive Ancient Agora Excavations • 50. Photographic Archive Museum of the Ancient Agora • 51. Photographic Archive Archaeological Receipts Fund (TAPA) • 52. Photographic Archive Ancient Agora Excavations • 53. Photographic Archive A.P. Matthaiou (photo. I EPCA) • 54. Photographic Archive A.P. Matthaiou (photo. I EPCA) • 55. Photographic Archive A.P. Matthaiou (photo. Epigraphic Museum) • 56. Photographic Archive M. TOUBIS Publishing House • 57. Photographic Archive EKDOTIKE ATHENON • 58. Photo. N. Daniilidis • 59, 60. Photographic Archive MELISSA Publishing House • 61. Photographic Archive NAM (photo. Y. Patrikianos) • 63. Photographic Archive Antikenmuseum, Staatliche Museen Preußischer Kulturbesitz, Berlin • 64–66. Photographic Archive III EPCA (photo. S. Mavrommatis) • 67. Photographic Archive M. Korres • 68. Photographic Archive New Acropolis Museum (photo. S. Mavrommatis) • 69–72. Photo. S. Mavrommatis • 73. Photo. S. Daniilidis • 74, 75. Photographic Archive III EPCA • 76. Photographic Archive M. TOUBIS Publishing House • 77. Photographic Archive III EPCA (photo. S. Mavrommatis) • 78. Photographic Archive M. TOUBIS Publishing House • 79, 80. Photographic Archive NAM (photo. Y. Patrikianos) • 81, 82. Photographic Archive M. TOUBIS Publishing House • 83. Photographic Archive New Acropolis Museum (photo. S. Mavrommatis) • 84. Photographic Archive Organization for the Construction of the New Acropolis Museum (photo. N. Daniilidis) • 85. Photographic Archive Ancient Agora Excavations • 86, 87. Photo. S. Mavrommatis • 88. Acropolis Restoration Service • 89. Photographic Archive NAM (photo. Y. Patrikianos) • 90. Photo. N. Daniilidis • 91, 93. Photographic Archive L. Palaiokrassa-Kopitsa • 92. Photographic Archive II EPCA • 94. Photo. G. Kouroupis • 95. Photographic Archive NAM (photo. C. Xenikakis) • 96. Photographic Archive Ancient Agora Excavations • 97, 98. Photographic Archive Photostock-K. Kontos • 99. Photographic Archive Archaeological Receipts Fund (TAPA) • 100. Photographic Archive Rijksmuseum van Oudheden, Leiden • 101. Photographic Archive Photostock-K. Kontos • 102–104. Photographic Archive III EPCA (photo. G. Asvestas) • 105. Photo. S. Mavrommatis • 106. Photographic Archive Royal Ontario Museum, ©ROM • 107. Photo. S. Mavrommatis • 108. Photographic Archive NAM • 109. Photographic Archive G. Despinis • 110. Photo. G. Kouroupis • 111. Photographic Archive MELISSA Publishing House • 112. Photo. G. Kouroupis • 113. Photographic Archive NAM (photo. Y. Patrikianos) • 114, 116. Photographic Archive MELISSA Publishing House • 115. Photo. S. Mavrommatis • 117. Acropolis Restoration Service • 117. Acropolis Restoration Service (photo. V. Eleftheriou) • 119. Photographic Archive NAM (photo. Y. Patrikianos) • 122, 123. Photographic Archive MELISSA Publishing House • 124. Photographic Archive NAM (photo. I. Miari) • 125. Photo. A. Vlachopoulos • 126. Photographic Archive NAM • 127, 128. Photo. G. Kouroupis • 129, 131. Photographic Archive MELISSA Publishing House • 133. Photographic Archive Ancient Agora Excavations • 134–136. Photographic Archive II EPCA (photo. S. Mavrommatis) • 137. Photographic Archive Ephorate of East Attica • 138. Photographic Archive XXVI EPCA • 139. Photographic Archive MELISSA Publishing House • 141. Photographic Archive Epigraphic Museum • 142. Photographic Archive II EPCA (photo. C. Xenikakis) • 143. Photographic Archive II EPCA • 144, 145. Photo. G. Kouroupis • 146–148. Photographic Archive Archaeological Receipts Fund (TAPA) • 149. Photographic Archive Merenda Excavations, II EPCA • 150. Photo. G. Kouroupis • 151. Photographic Archive G. Steinhauer • 152. Photographic Archive NAM (photo. I. Miari) • 153. Photographic Archive D. Schilardi (II EPCA) • 154. Photographic Archive XXVI EPCA • 155. Photographic Archive II EPCA • 156, 157. Photographic Archive XXVI EPCA (photo. G. Kouragios) • 158. Photographic Archive G. Steinhauer • 159–163. Photographic Archive Merenda Excavations, II EPCA • 164. Photographic Archive Antikensammlungen, Munich • 165. Photographic Archive II EPCA • 166. Photographic Archive II EPCA • 167. Photographic Archive II EPCA (photo. C. Xenikakis) • 168. Photographic Archive Museum of Fine Arts, Boston • 169. Photographic Archive XXVI EPCA • 170. Photographic Archive Merenda Excavations, II EPCA • 171. Photographic Archive II EPCA (photo. C. Xenikakis) • 172–177. Photographic Archive XXVI EPCA • 178, 179. Photographic Archive Danish Archaeological Institute • 180–183. Photographic Archive XXVI EPCA